THIS IS WHERE YOUR HEALING BEGINS

THIS IS WHERE YOUR HEALING BEGINS

NIGEL W.D. MUMFORD

EMANATE
BOOKS

Published in Nashville, Tennessee, by Emanate Books, an imprint of Thomas Nelson. Emanate Books and Thomas Nelson are registered trademarks of HarperCollins Christian Publishing, Inc.

Thomas Nelson titles may be purchased in bulk for educational, business, fund-raising, or sales promotional use. For information, please e-mail SpecialMarkets@ThomasNelson.com.

Unless otherwise noted, Scripture quotations are taken from the Holy Bible, New International Version®, NIV®. Copyright © 1973, 1978, 1984, 2011 by Biblica, Inc.® Used by permission of Zondervan. All rights reserved worldwide. www.Zondervan.com. The "NIV" and "New International Version" are trademarks registered in the United States Patent and Trademark Office by Biblica, Inc.®

Scripture quotations marked ESV are from the ESV® Bible (The Holy Bible, English Standard Version®). Copyright © 2001 by Crossway, a publishing ministry of Good News Publishers. Used by permission. All rights reserved.

Scripture quotations marked KJV are from the King James Version. Public domain.

Scripture quotations marked THE MESSAGE are from *The Message*. Copyright © by Eugene H. Peterson 1993, 1994, 1995, 1996, 2000, 2001, 2002. Used by permission of NavPress. All rights reserved. Represented by Tyndale House Publishers, Inc.

Scripture quotations marked NLT are from the Holy Bible, New Living Translation. © 1996, 2004, 2007, 2013, 2015 by Tyndale House Foundation. Used by permission of Tyndale House Publishers, Inc., Carol Stream, Illinois 60188. All rights reserved.

Scripture quotations marked RSV are from Revised Standard Version of the Bible. Copyright 1946, 1952, and 1971 National Council of the Churches of Christ in the United States of America. Used by permission. All rights reserved.

Scripture quotations marked AMP are from the Amplified® Bible. Copyright © 1954, 1958, 1962, 1964, 1965, 1987 by The Lockman Foundation. Used by permission. (www.Lockman.org)

ISBN 978-0-7852-3318-3 (eBook)
ISBN 978-0-7852-3316-9 (TP)

Library of Congress Control Number:2019952653

Printed in the United States of America
20 21 22 23 24 LSC 10 9 8 7 6 5 4 3 2 1

CONTENTS

This book is dedicated to
Dr. Francis and Judith MacNutt
For the years of friendship, mentoring, and
joy in the vineyard of the Lord.
Thank you for your extraordinary kindness.
You are both very dear souls.

FOREWORD

Nigel Mumford and I go back a long way, and I have enormous respect for him as a person and for his remarkable ministry of healing and deliverance. We are all unique—God doesn't do duplicates—but I can't help but feel that Nigel is in some way more unique than others. He defies pigeonholing, categorization, and sometimes the rulebook: for an Anglican minister he can be distinctly un-Anglican, and I like that. Yet he is a man of God and does extraordinary things in the name of Jesus, and that's good enough for me.

The theme of this book has to do with practicing the ministry of healing and the miraculous healings that result from such a ministry. Frankly, that presents a challenge not just to me but to every Christian. Almost all of us agree that miracles occur today, but there are aspects that are far from straightforward. The miraculous or supernatural restoration of health raises many questions. Why do some people have the gift of healing and others not? Why can a single, simple prayer heal one sick person and the fervent prayers of thousands be ineffective for another? How do we balance prayer for healing and modern medicine? How important is our faith in seeing a cure happen? Is miraculous healing a rare exception or something we should expect more frequently?

I have no easy answers to these and other questions, and I'm wary of those who do. I do not have the gift of healing, and I suspect it is far more widely claimed than genuinely present. Nigel, however, is one of the few people I know who genuinely does have the gift of healing and has, over many years, not just spoken on it but also practiced it with remarkable results. As a former Royal Marine, Nigel knows that two sorts of people write about war: the academics who have never strayed from their desks and the soldiers who were there on the battle-front. This is a book from the front line; this is Nigel's territory. He has "walked the talk," and I'm prepared to listen to what he has to say.

As it pertains to healing and the related subjects raised here, I feel that any treatment of them needs to have a number of characteristics.

First, it needs to be stimulating. It's often supposed that facts give rise to belief. In fact, the reality is more complex: what we believe influences what we accept to be facts. And with healing and other related areas, it's easy to let our own particular theological position govern how we see things. Nigel—ever a man to wade in and act while everybody else stands by, discussing what they should do—asks questions, challenges assumptions, and proposes alternatives. Who else but Nigel would encourage us to give thanks to God as we take our medicine? (And, by the way, why not?) It's hard not to read this book without pausing to consider our own opinion on such matters. You will no doubt find yourself asking that very useful question: Is what I've always believed actually the truth?

Second, it needs to be sensitive. A great deal of harm has been done not just to individuals but to the name of Christ by reckless, clumsy, and sometimes exaggerated claims about healing. Healing is not magic done for the praise of the practitioner or even the benefit of the church but for the restoration to health of individual men and women whom God cares for deeply. Love and grace must be present. Here, too, this book scores strongly: Nigel retains a pastoral heart in what he does and says.

Third, any discussion of these matters needs to be sensible. How do we balance prayer and prescriptions, miracles and medicine, the works of the Spirit and those of the surgeon? We are all aware of horror stories of individuals who, trusting in prayer, have thrown away their medicines with dreadful consequences. How do we deal with the complex relationship between body, mind, and spirit? Again, Nigel—a veteran of hospital treatment himself—treads carefully and wisely.

Finally, any discussion needs to be scriptural. With respect to healing and these other matters, God's Word gives us a framework that we must work within. It sets limits beyond which we must not go: for example, we must never put healing of the body above our relationship with God. Yet it also sets goals for the practice of healing: it must all be done to the praise and glory of Father, Son, and Spirit. Here, too, Nigel is surefooted and keeps the focus on God.

To be honest, after reading this book I'm not sure that I don't find myself with more questions than I had at the start. There is much that I'm still evaluating and that I need to think further about, but that is no bad thing. God's dealings with us should never be reduced to simple formulae. Yet this book reinforces two vital truths. The first is that we do not understand everything to do with how the body (let alone soul and spirit) actually works. Here, arrogance is folly and humility is wisdom. The second and far more important truth is that Christ, our living Lord, is the Great Physician capable of healing all our ills. We need to hold on to both, and this book is an encouragement to do just that.

J. JOHN
REVEREND CANON

INTRODUCTION

For more than thirty years I have listened, loved, and prayed for healing over thousands of people. I've seen countless supplicants (those earnestly seeking healing) healed from a variety of needs of everyday life—disease, depression, doubt, shame, guilt, generational curses, and all other manner of human pain and suffering.

The wisdom I have gained from this experience is contained in this book. It has come from being tethered to God's Word and His Holy Spirit and presents for you, dear Christian reader, biblical instructions for how you, too, can become a healing minister. I listen intently to God as I pray for every precious soul. Every person responds uniquely to my initial query: *"How may I pray for you?"* From these interactions, I've witnessed Christ's creativity. Every supplicant for whom I've prayed has taught me something new, or *anew*—another facet of the gem of His boundless love for us. This can be your experience as well.

Whether these interactions have taken place in a classroom, the trenches, a prayer room, a chapel, the post office, a nursing home, a hospital, on an airplane, or by telephone, God has prevailed upon me that I must decrease so that He may increase (John 3:30). To ensure that there is absolutely no confusion, I want to say up front that I am not a healer—God alone is the Healer.

As I come alongside those who are seeking healing, I recognize the brilliance of the adage "Our adversities are God's universities." My classroom is without walls or roofs. My classroom is embodied in the very soul of the person seeking healing, either sitting or standing in front of me. As I pray, God's Holy Spirit helps me to wonder: *What can I learn from this supplicant that can also help the next person I encounter? What can I understand, grasp, and take away from this supplicant's unique situation that can offer insight into helping others?*

There is no college or seminary course available that can provide one answer to the countless diverse causes and needs for healing human lives. Every soul is unique. Thus, the human needs for healing and the peculiar personal histories surrounding them are numerous and multifaceted. The felt needs shared with me most every day involve physical, emotional, mental, spiritual, generational, identity, relational, financial, historical, locational, racial, interdenominational, intellectual, and other universal issues of healing. These needs arise out of, but are not limited to, physical illness, sexual and verbal abuse, traumas, spiritual and family dysfunction, abandonment, shame, guilt, rejection, doubt, fear, and anxiety.

Tragically, and too often, I encounter the residual bitterness, resentment, and painful scars of transgressions that supplicants suffered decades earlier in their childhood and youth. Now, many years later, as they seek healing prayer, their wounds may even be disguised as a "mask" of a mental or physical diagnosed illness. In either case, as I pray for God to meet the need, very often I discover the underlying cause of their illness to be a decades-old dis-*ease*. It becomes clear that old wounds have caused their illness. Following prayer there is often a visible change in their countenance as their burdens are surrendered to Jesus. I frequently see a "fist of resentment" completely relax as their emotional or physical pain is surrendered to Christ. It is always a privilege when we can see God at work within the lives of those over whom we have prayed.

In 1990, when God first led me into His ministry of healing, supplicants would regularly tell me, "I've come here as a last resort." In the early days the majority of those who sought prayer were females over the age of fifty. However, now the demographics have greatly expanded. Today, men, women, and children of all ages—believers and nonbelievers—come for prayer. I actually met with someone who blatantly declared, "Thank God I'm an atheist!" After our prayer, he did not remain an atheist for much longer!

While it is more likely for those in need to make a beeline from their doctor's office to mine, it is becoming increasingly common for people to come for prayer in advance of visiting their physician's office. As supplicants experience God's healing gifts in Christ Jesus, the words of the psalmist begin to resonate with them: "I remain confident of this: I will see the goodness of the LORD in the land of the living" (Psalm 27:13). Hence becoming filled with faith in the Healer leads people to a greater certainty of God's loving-kindness and to be more apt to include Him in every aspect of their healing. It is no surprise that when medical concerns arise, followers of Christ pray before seeing a doctor. If only more doctors understood that faith-filled people know that God, as their ultimate Healer, also creatively heals through doctors, medicines, and technology. I am told of several doctors who even write prescriptions for their patients to attend healing services and receive prayer.

Jesus commanded His disciples to "heal the sick" (Matthew 10:8). Today, you and I are His disciples. The wisdom God has given us is to never limit Him. God can do far more than we could ever ask or imagine! As we journey through this book, my prayer is that you will be inspired to dive into the Holy Scriptures to explore and appropriate His healing gifts for yourselves and for all those you care about—that this is where your healing ministry begins.

Be well, do good works, and for the sake of God, love one another!

THE REV. NIGEL W. D. MUMFORD
VIRGINIA BEACH, VIRGINIA

Part One

FOUNDATIONS OF HEALING

GIFTS

Now eagerly desire the greater gifts.
—1 CORINTHIANS 12:31

The Quandary

Let me say quite clearly, I am not a healer. Nor am I a faith healer: only God heals.

Perhaps the overarching question should be, "Is it 'faith healing' or 'faith in God's ability to heal'?" If the sick person must exercise faith, then how much faith did Lazarus have to be healed? Because John 11:39 makes it undoubtedly clear that he was already dead! "'Take away the stone,' he [Jesus] said. 'But, Lord,' said Martha, the sister of the dead man, 'by this time there is a bad odor, for he has been there four days.'" More often we find faith in Christ's ability and willingness to heal present in the one who prays for a supplicant and not necessarily in the supplicant who receives prayer.

And yet, we would be remiss to discount the story of the woman who was healed from twelve years of hemorrhaging blood (Matthew 9:20–22; Mark 5:25–34; Luke 8:43–48) yet demonstrated astounding faith in Jesus' healing gifts. But that's not so in every case.

So, whether you have unwavering faith or no faith at all, Jesus can still heal! I have witnessed both circumstances—time and time again.

Successful Prayer?

I am sometimes asked, "What is your success rate?" I respond that my success rate is zero, but God has an amazing success percentage. In support of my answer, I point out the biblical story of the ten lepers. Though ten were cured, only one was truly healed. As Jesus had instructed, all ten cured lepers went to show themselves to the priest, but only one returned of his own volition to thank Jesus.

The one who gave thanks was cured not only in his body but also in his mind and spirit! The grateful one recognized and acknowledged Christ as his Healer. An "attitude of gratitude" is foremost in the hearts, minds, and spirits of those who have been healed.

For nearly two decades, from 1990 to 2009, the prayer of the father with the epileptic son, found in Mark 9:24—"I do believe; help me overcome my unbelief"—had regularly been my own prayer. "Lord, I do believe, but heal my unbelief" was my personal pivotal petition. But in 2009, that all changed.

My Own Healing

I became critically ill with the H1N1 swine flu virus in October 2009. After months of hospitalization, I awoke from a lengthy coma and my doctor said, "I have never seen anyone so close to death and not die as you!" This white-haired Vietnam combat physician had witnessed death and dying too often during his military service. So, his declaration of my "resurrection" caused me to make my own declaration of faith from that day forward. Whenever I'm confronted with a personal need for healing or a situation that requires my decision to either choose to be at peace or to be anxious (panic), I declare without reservation, "Lord, I believe!" Why? Because I have been healed. I have had my own Lazarus experience.

Despite having seen so many people healed by God during my healing ministry, when it was my turn to be desperately ill, it was unmistakably Jesus Christ who had healed me. Since then I have known that I would never again need to pray against my own unbelief. Christ's healing gifts are now intensely personal to me—they are undeniably, inescapably real!

A Minister of Healing

So then, because you have bought this book, I imagine that you, too, believe it is possible for you and those you hope to pray for to tap into such confidence and spiritual rootedness that defeats fear and doubt. But it would be human to doubt just a little. After all, we are talking about God working miracles and the supernatural breaking through into the natural world. There is a great mystery here. Nevertheless, my prayer is that as you read through this book, you will allow His Spirit and truth to wash over you and drown any obstacles that exist to prevent or curtail your steadfast belief in Him and His greater gifts and your ability to use them for His glory in a healing ministry.

How do you get started? Well, a good place is to focus on three foundational Bible verses pertaining to healing.

The first is Luke 9:2, which says, "And he [Jesus] sent them out to proclaim the kingdom of God and to heal the sick." Though the modern church appears to be doing the task of preaching and proclaiming the kingdom, it has generally failed to exercise its ministry to heal the sick. I encourage you to read again this short verse from the gospel of Luke as a charge from Jesus to His disciples. Is that charge still relevant today? Does your church have a healing ministry or healing prayer group that meets? Have you even considered that Jesus Christ's healing gifts are still available today?

The second foundational healing verse is an extension of Luke 9:2

and is found in Matthew 10, providing more detailed instructions: "As you go, proclaim this message: 'The kingdom of heaven has come near. Heal the sick, raise the dead, cleanse those who have leprosy, drive out demons. Freely you have received; freely give'" (vv. 7–8). Friends, these are our marching orders from Jesus Himself. How often do we encounter them inside or outside of our churches? Where are believers, today, who have faith akin to that of the centurion as found in Matthew 8?

> When Jesus had entered Capernaum, a centurion came to him, asking for help. "Lord," he said, "my servant lies at home paralyzed, suffering terribly."
>
> Jesus said to him, "Shall I come and heal him?"
>
> The centurion replied, "Lord, I do not deserve to have you come under my roof. But just say the word, and my servant will be healed. For I myself am a man under authority, with soldiers under me. I tell this one, 'Go,' and he goes; and that one, 'Come,' and he comes. I say to my servant, 'Do this,' and he does it."
>
> When Jesus heard this, he was amazed and said to those following him, "Truly I tell you, I have not found anyone in Israel with such great faith." (vv. 5–10)

As a veteran of military service, specifically as a drill instructor of fifty uniformed men, it was my job to teach those recruits to kill or be killed. When I read the above account, I completely understood how readily this soldier recognized and honored Jesus' authority. An ironic aside: due to life's unexpected twists and turns, it is my privilege today to teach people to heal and be healed. I used to make grown men cry as a drill instructor; I still do as a priest.

The third foundational passage I want to underscore are Paul's words: "After the reading from the Law and the Prophets, the leaders of the synagogue sent word to them, saying, 'Brothers, if you have a word of exhortation for the people, please speak'" (Acts 13:15).

A word of exhortation is generally an encouragement for the hearer. As such, my prayer is that this book will be a profound message of encouragement from our Lord for each of you.

It Is Finished!

At the beginning of Holy Communion (also called the Eucharist or Great Thanksgiving), the celebrant commands, "Lift up your hearts," to which the congregation responds, "We lift them to the Lord."

As I approach those in need of healing, I remind myself that the person requesting prayer (the supplicant) is a soul who has been placed in my care for just a short while. Too often in that moment I can feel the crush of their self-condemnation. Oh, that all supplicants would know that Jesus has already been nailed to the cross—on their behalves. Truly, it is finished! Jesus died once, for all, for all time. Even if it were possible to sacrifice ourselves as He did, it would have no bearing on us or on anyone else. Jesus Christ alone, as the incarnation of our triune God, was the only perfect sacrifice, and He has already done it—for us. There is nothing left to do, dear people, but to say, "Thanks be to God!"

Through the Lord's Eyes

When I engage in healing prayer for a supplicant or lead a healing service or mission, I ask the Lord to allow me to decrease so that He may increase. I ask Him to deliver me from "my stuff" and fill me with all of Him. I surrender my knowledge, my experience, my judgment, and my thinking to Him so that He can have His way through my obedience.

When I approach a supplicant, I choose to see that person in my mind's eye as already healed by God. It is important for me to find the felt, or targeted, need of the supplicant and to possess Christ's understanding of his or her concerns. I see my prayers as laser beams, like a holy scalpel, targeting their needs.

Whether the supplicant has a physical, emotional, historical, mental, or spiritual need for healing, my prayer of faith is always a gentle command filled with faith, power, and expectancy. No need to shout. God is not deaf. He delights in the voices of His children as they bring their concerns to Him. He knows better than any the histories and backgrounds of all who petition Him. And whenever two or three are gathered in His name, He is present.

Imagine Michelangelo contemplating a block of marble as he envisions what will be revealed when he has finished sculpting. In some respects, supplicants are akin to blocks of marble. As prayer for a supplicant begins, sometimes those praying are able to see beyond, through Christ's eyes, to the healed person after their sickness is cut out. I believe that Jesus saw deep into the souls of those for whom He prayed, seeing their healed souls just beyond their veil of dis-ease.

Hence, Jesus' own healing prayers, as recorded in the Bible, are filled with faith, power, and expectancy. The Lord sees everything through eternity. Please do not misunderstand me, however; I am certainly not advocating "name it and claim it." I am saying that if you believe Jesus is who He says He is and that He will do what He says He will do, then you will be not only free to receive healing prayer for yourself but also free to pray in faith, with power and expectancy, for others.

Anchors for Healing Prayer

Let's spend some time looking at supportive scripture and church tradition and other pertinent areas to help anchor us as we explore healing prayer more deeply.

Scripture

I encourage you to commit to spending time in the Holy Bible, reading all the stories of healing. If you have access to the internet, go to Biblegateway.com and search *heal, healed,* or *healing.* There are hundreds of verses in the Old and New Testaments that will pop up for you to digest. If you have never done this, you will be amazed at the gems you will find and how very busy Jesus was with healing while He walked this earth.

There is one passage, however, that you will find in your search that I would like to highlight here. I consider this to be at the epicenter of healing—almost a blueprint and foundation upon which the ministry of Christ's healing gifts is built. It is commonly called the Prayer of Faith:

> Is anyone among you in trouble? Let them pray. Is anyone happy?
> Let them sing songs of praise. Is anyone among you sick? Let them
> call the elders of the church to pray over them and anoint them with
> oil in the name of the Lord. And the prayer offered in faith will
> make the sick person well; the Lord will raise them up. If they have
> sinned, they will be forgiven. Therefore confess your sins to each
> other and pray for each other so that you may be healed. The prayer
> of a righteous person is powerful and effective. (James 5:13–16)

Won't you take time now to carefully read the above passage again? By the time you finish reading this book, the words of this prayer will breathe new life into you.

Tradition

"Jesus Christ is the same yesterday and today and forever" (Hebrews 13:8).

For Christ is the power and the glory forever and ever—no fabrication or exaggeration here. We were made in His image. It puzzles me that this truth and our tradition of worshipping Him, for more than two millennia, is balked at by each new generation. Why is that, I wonder? Why is there so much skepticism? Or have we been too sheltered from encountering the spiritual dullness that exists today?

The first time I was asked to teach a weeklong seminary course, I was unnerved when the professor pulled me out of class into the hall, after I was introduced and before I had even opened my mouth. He proceeded to share with me that the man at the back of the class—arms folded across his chest, glaring out the window—did not believe that God heals today and would be my greatest challenge. I feigned gratitude as I mustered courage to reenter the classroom and take my place at the podium. Desperately trying to divert my eyes from this man, I opened with prayer and launched into Healing 101.

Then, out of the blue, in the middle of my lesson, I heard myself say aloud, "Who here has a bad right elbow?"

There was a lengthy pause before, to my surprise, the man at the back of the class slowly raised his left hand! I asked if he had tennis elbow, and he replied, "Yes, how did you know?" I then asked him to kindly come forward to me. I also asked two other students who had been leaning into my talk to join us at the front.

I asked the man about the history of his elbow and asked his permission to lay hands on him in prayer, directing the other two to also lay their hands on him. Afterward, the man stared oddly at his elbow and slowly began to test his mobility. Gradually he enthusiastically, and more rapidly, worked his elbow. He demonstrated to the whole class that his elbow was healed! This chap became my star pupil for the rest of the week. God does work in mysterious ways and, when necessary, will woo even the greatest skeptic. His truth will always trump cynicism and doubt!

Reason

From the beginning, God gave us free will. The human brain He designed and created gives us the power to think, understand, and reason. With information we receive, we have the power to reason and form our own conclusions and judgments. When I first became involved in healing ministry, reason played an important part, but not any longer.

Though reason was a great tool to help me understand healing, my beliefs are no longer dependent on reason. Over the past decades, I've witnessed such astounding evidence of answered prayers that I have come to know that my Savior lives and that His healing gifts are at work this very day. I do not need to think it through any longer. Though God captured my attention through reason, I now rest in Christ and on the evidence itself. I did not arrive here aware of where I was headed; I only know that I used to be there, but now I am confidently here. The best news is that He can bring you here, too, beloved.

Feelings

"He may let them rest in a feeling of security, but his eyes are on their ways" (Job 24:23).

Feelings are tricky in our spiritual life. For the most part, any emotion—whether joy or jealousy, comfort or chaos—can be effectively vetted as we grow deeper and more closely identify with Jesus Christ. We are more in tune with God and able to avoid ascribing to God the varied and deceptive feelings we sometimes have in our flesh.

Emotions run the gamut in healing ministry. They are raw and palpable in the person who is sick and in need of healing. As human beings we understand how highly charged some circumstances are in others' lives, as well as in our own. However, "feelings" are not reliable, nor are they helpful to the one(s) praying for the sick person. If feelings get the upper hand of those who pray for the sick, faith-filled prayers will be distorted by sympathy, sorrow, rejection, revulsion, and other human emotions. Should that occur, the guidance of the Holy Spirit and Christ's power are muted as dramatically as they are when doubt or fear rule us.

When prayer ministers' faith is cemented in the certainty of God's power, grace, and loving-kindness, they are better able to hear Him direct their prayers and obey what they hear from Him, rather than defer to their emotions.

Thinking

Thinking all this through can be totally overwhelming. Not unlike reason in many respects, thinking can be more insidious because although we may not be drawing conclusions or judgments, the time spent thinking on our own is time spent away from listening to God for His narrative.

I prefer "blind faith," or total faith. Not ignorant faith, but child-like. Having blind faith allows the Lord to lead us and reveal His truths to us. When we exercise blind faith, we will see with His eyes precisely what He wants us to know. Isaiah 42:16 tells us, "I will lead the blind by ways they have not known, along unfamiliar paths I will guide them; I will turn the darkness into light before them and make the rough places smooth. These are the things I will do; I will not forsake them." Would you rather a healing prayer minister be led by his or her own thinking or by your heavenly Father's vision of you?

Inspired healing prayer for the sick is founded in the certainty that when Christ is asked, He will answer, and the sick for whom we pray will receive what God intends, not what we healing prayer ministers think is necessary.

"And this is the confidence we have in approaching God: that if we ask anything according to his will, he hears us. And if we know that *he hears* us—whatever *we ask*—we know that *we have* what we asked of him" (1 John 5:14–15, emphasis added).

Reread the above passage from John's first letter. Look at the six italicized words . . . He hears, we ask, we have. There is so much packed into these two verses, but please do not miss the astounding goodness of God when we pray to Him in accordance with His will. Is healing the will of God? Does God want to heal us? Oh yes, beloved—He is unstoppable because Jesus Christ is, Himself, healing. But more about that later.

Action

Action should always follow obedience. When the Lord stirs in the sick person, he will ask to be prayed for. When he indicates his desire to receive prayer, prayer ministers then act and respond to the sick person, "How may I pray for you?"

This is the starting point, the point at which the sick person and his prayer minister take the dis-ease and place it at Christ's feet. Oftentimes the supplicant takes this opportunity to share a bit of his history, though it is not always necessary because the Lord already knows and is able to impart that knowledge to the prayer minister directly.

The next action occurs when the sick person is asked by the prayer minister, "May I lay my hands on you in prayer?" When I ask this question of supplicants, I simultaneously and silently pray to the Lord: *May my hands be Your hands, Lord.*

Finally, it is very important to know that something always happens when we pray. When a sick person surrenders to healing prayer and receives prayer from those who are surrendered to God's authority and His Holy Spirit, the Lord will move and we will receive.

While reading this book, you may be drawn to pray for others for the first time. Praise God if you do! But take care to never compare the need of a supplicant with the needs of anyone else, including your own. Be careful not to talk about yourself, as this can happen if you are keeping your own counsel in prayer or are over-relating to the disease or dis-ease the supplicant has shared. Your objective is to *agape*, love selflessly, the person for whom you are praying (whether silently or aloud). Get out of God's way so He can use you by infusing His Word into any diseased tissue in body, mind, or spirit. Apply His Word in prayer like a poultice, letting Him permeate the source of the need, saturating each cell until the supplicant is immersed in His healing gifts.

HOLY SPIRIT

There are different kinds of gifts, but
the same Spirit distributes them.
—1 CORINTHIANS 12:4

The Holy Spirit and prayer are like the wind. You can't see them, but you can certainly see what they do.

Jesus answered, "Very truly I tell you, no one can enter the kingdom of God unless they are born of water and the Spirit. Flesh gives birth to flesh, but the Spirit gives birth to spirit. You should not be surprised at my saying, 'You must be born again.' The wind blows wherever it pleases. You hear its sound, but you cannot tell where it comes from or where it is going. So it is with everyone born of the Spirit." (John 3:5–8)

Some years ago I was in a church sanctuary in Boston teaching on the healing ministry, and I made a sweeping gesture with my hand over the seventy-five or so people in the class. I can't remember what led up to it or what I was saying at the moment, but I remember it in slow motion. With my left hand I reached over to my right shoulder and with an outstretched arm and open hand moved my left hand through the air over everyone in the sanctuary.

To my utter amazement, everyone—the whole group—slumped in the pews. The entire gathering was resting in the Spirit! It was as if they had all instantly fallen asleep. Holy peace had descended upon everyone. It was astonishing.

Just two people were left standing: Rena, the woman standing beside me who had invited me to speak, and me. Rena looked at me and asked, "Now what do we do?" Smiling, I replied, "I suppose we just let them rest." Then, of course, she and I fell out laughing with joy. I had seen this sort of thing occur on television, but never up close and in my proximity. What had just happened? On the one hand, it was exhilarating, but on the other hand it was so extraordinary that I confess to you I felt slightly terrified. It was a memorable healing experience with loads of blessings for all who attended.

"One day Jesus was teaching, and Pharisees and teachers of the law were sitting there. . . . And the power of the Lord was with Jesus to heal the sick" (Luke 5:17). This verse comes to mind as it points to yet another passage in which Jesus is quoted as saying:

> Very truly I tell you, whoever believes in me will do the works I have been doing, and they will do even greater things than these, because I am going to the Father. And I will do whatever you ask in my name, so that the Father may be glorified in the Son. You may ask me for anything in my name, and I will do it. If you love me, keep my commands. And I will ask the Father, and he will give you another advocate to help you and be with you forever—the Spirit of truth. The world cannot accept him, because it neither sees him nor knows him. But you know him, for he lives with you and will be in you. (John 14:12–17)

You see, the whole gathering that was resting (or "slain") in the Spirit had nothing in particular to do with me, Nigel Mumford. It had everything to do with my 1) belief in Him, 2) His gift of the Holy

Spirit indwelling me, 3) His command to obey, and 4) His promise that, through the Holy Spirit in me, He "will do even greater things than these"!

Of course, it is often difficult to believe for something that we have never been taught. That is not a new phenomenon. In Acts we glimpse the disciples spending time explaining and enlightening those who did not know what and how Jesus did what He did:

> You know what has happened throughout the province of Judea, beginning in Galilee after the baptism that John preached— how God anointed Jesus of Nazareth with the Holy Spirit and power, and how he went around doing good and healing all who were under the power of the devil, because God was with him. (10:37–38)

We mustn't forget that the primary gift of the Holy Spirit is the Holy Spirit Himself. Until Jesus' crucifixion, death, resurrection, and ascension into heaven, the Holy Spirit only lived among us, not in us. However, after Jesus ascended to the throne, He sat down at the Father's right hand and asked the Father to give us "another advocate to help you and be with you forever." Now the Holy Spirit dwells inside us forever!

To know the presence of the Holy Spirit during a healing service or prayer session is positively thrilling. It is such a joy and privilege to meet with God in this way. One can sense His power and glory being poured out over those in need of healing. It is a palpable feeling—a sort of knowing or quickening in the atmosphere around you. Such times cannot be forced and are certainly not subject to God's performance upon our command. One can simply invite the Holy Spirit to join in and know that He most likely will. Other times, I find that the Holy Spirit surprises us and just shows up! Praising and worshipping the Lord in music and in word are important displays in which we indicate to Him how very welcome He is. It is always important that the atmosphere or environment surrounding our time with God is inviting. Paul wrote: "May the God of hope fill you with all joy and peace as you trust in him, so that you may overflow with hope by the power of the Holy Spirit" (Romans 15:13).

It pleases the Holy Spirit when we trust Him. Obedience is another pleasing offering to Him. Acts 15 contains serious rifts in the early church that arose out of teachings on the essentials of salvation. Some believers were adding prerequisites to salvation that did not reflect God's nature. Thus, a council meeting in Jerusalem was held. Paul and Barnabas joined James, Peter, and others there for an open exchange of understanding and ideas. After some time, James addressed the assembly and set forth a pared-down list of behaviors to be avoided in anticipation of salvation. Before presenting those behaviors, James prefaced the list with the following decree: "It seemed good to the Holy Spirit . . ." (Acts 15:28).

Indeed, when it seems good to the Holy Spirit, we can know that we have left the door open for Him to come in. During such times we can almost see a great big, glorious welcome mat on our doorstep, beckoning Him to come in and make His home within us. Trusting, praising, worshipping, and obeying Him are the signposts of welcome that the Holy Spirit looks for in us—His temples. First Corinthians 6:19–20 says: "Do you not know that your bodies are temples of the Holy Spirit, who is in you, whom you have received from God? You are not your own; you were bought at a price."

There is a wonderful story about a man who died and went to heaven. St. Peter said to him, "I have some time until the next group arrives. Come with me." They walked together on the gold cobblestones of heaven's streets and finally arrived at a warehouse. Inside he saw countless shelves. St. Peter pointed to one shelf and said, "This is your shelf." The shelf was crowded with gift-wrapped boxes. "What's this?" the man asked. St. Peter replied, "Those are the gifts God wanted you to have, which you never asked for." This just screams of James 4:2, doesn't it? "You do not have because you do not ask God."

It is my heart's desire that you know, believe, and think with the mind of Christ so that you can expand your faith to believe your amazing, unfathomable God in all three of His glorious personalities—God the Father; God the Son, Jesus Christ; and God the Holy Spirit. In 1 Corinthians Paul is clear about God wanting to give you the gifts of the Holy Spirit.

Chapter 12 begins, "Now about the gifts of the Spirit, brothers and sisters, I do not want you to be uninformed."

The Message translation of the same verse says, "What I want to talk about now is the various ways God's Spirit gets worked into our lives. This is complex and often misunderstood, but I want you to be informed and knowledgeable."

And the King James Version is translated as, "Now concerning spiritual gifts, brethren, I would not have you ignorant."

Are you getting the picture here? How much plainer could Paul make it? He wants all brothers and sisters, those who follow Christ as Lord and Savior, to be informed and knowledgeable about the gifts—no uncertainty about it. Even if your Christian faith-base, for whatever possible reason, does not believe that the gifts of the Holy Spirit are in play today, be assured that St. Paul wanted us to know about them so that we are not ignorant.

So, what are these gifts?

While Paul's "list" in 1 Corinthians 12 may begin in verse 8, don't skim over verses 4–6 and verse 7. Remember Paul's quote—that the working of the gifts of the Holy Spirit are complex and often misunderstood. No speed-reading!

First Corinthians 12:4–6 says, "There are different kinds of gifts, but the same Spirit distributes them. There are different kinds of service, but the same Lord. There are different kinds of working, but in all of them and in everyone it is the same God at work."

Verse 7 is a single "tour de verse." It corrects the notion that the gifts of the Holy Spirit are given to "you" or to "me." It is not about us, individually. They are for all! "Now to each one the manifestation of the Spirit is given for the common good."

The following passages from 1 Corinthians, Romans, and Ephesians list the gifts of the Spirit:

> To one there is given through the Spirit a message of wisdom, to another a message of knowledge by means of the same Spirit, to another faith by the same Spirit, to another gifts of healing by that one Spirit, to another miraculous powers, to another prophecy, to another distinguishing between spirits, to another speaking in different kinds of tongues, and to still another the interpretation of tongues. (1 Corinthians 12:8–10)

> Now you are the body of Christ, and each one of you is a part of it. And God has placed in the church first of all apostles, second prophets, third teachers, then miracles, then gifts of healing, of helping, of guidance, and of different kinds of tongues. (1 Corinthians 12:27–28)

> We have different gifts, according to the grace given to each of us. If your gift is prophesying, then prophesy in accordance with your faith; if it is serving, then serve; if it is teaching, then teach; if it is to encourage, then give encouragement; if it is giving, then give generously; if it is to lead, do it diligently; if it is to show mercy, do it cheerfully. (Romans 12:6–8)

> So Christ himself gave the apostles, the prophets, the evangelists, the pastors and teachers, to equip his people for works of service, so that the body of Christ may be built up. (Ephesians 4:11–12)

Now let's consolidate the lists found in these letters from St. Paul, eliminating duplicates and including their other commonly used names:

Message of wisdom (words of)
Message of knowledge (words of)
Faith
Gifts of healing(s)
Miraculous powers (miracles)
Distinguishing between spirits/guidance (discernment)
Speaking in different kinds of tongues (tongues / prayer languages)
Interpretation of tongues
Prophecy / prophesying
Encourage (encouragement, exhorting, exhortation)
Giving (generosity)
Showing mercy (mercy)
Helping / serving (helps, service)
Lead (leadership) and teaching

Five "offices" are also found within these lists: apostles, prophets, evangelists, pastors, and teachers.

Popular Christian understanding of the gifts could expand this list to include (as drawn from other scriptures) such other gifts of the Spirit as: administration, evangelism, intercession, martyrdom, hospitality, and craftsmanship. I would personally like to add: laughter, weeping, and groaning, all of which are gifts that enable us to express our Lord's heart and nature.

From reading Paul's letters we are told that God distributes each of these gifts just as He determines. Oftentimes we hear teaching that God gives us "a" (one) gift, but in my experience, God gives us any and all of these gifts as He equips us to accomplish His purposes. One of my favorite verses is often overlooked: "Now eagerly desire the greater gifts" (1 Corinthians 12:31). God tells us to actively seek, desire, and even ask for His gifts. The thing that all these gifts have in common is they help others. When we get away from our "me's" and "I's" and every hint of self-aggrandizement and self-entitlement, we're equipped and free to help others as God intended, and we'll see amazing healing take place—not only within us, but in others.

It is stunning to contemplate the value we have in God's gift of the Holy Spirit. Recall the story of Simon:

> Now . . . a man named Simon had practiced sorcery in the city and amazed all the people of Samaria . . . and all the people, both high and low, gave him their attention and exclaimed, "This man is rightly called the Great Power of God." They followed him. . . . But when they believed Philip as he proclaimed the good news of the . . . name of Jesus Christ, they were baptized. . . . Simon himself believed and was baptized. And he followed Philip . . . astonished by the great signs and miracles. (Acts 8:9–13)

But then we read on in verses 18–21:

> When Simon saw that the Spirit was given at the laying on of the apostles' hands, he offered them money and said, "Give me also this ability so that everyone on whom I lay my hands may receive the Holy Spirit." Peter answered: "May your money perish with you, because you thought you could buy the gift of God with money! You have no part or share in this ministry, because your heart is not right before God."

The gifts of the Holy Spirit are indeed that—gifts—and they cannot be purchased, nor can they be earned. They are gifts—free gifts. They are distributed by God's grace to whomever and whenever the Holy Spirit decides. Though gifts may not abide in you forever, they are always available to you for God's purposes. We must always, in receiving these gifts, give thanks!

I have been encouraging our own healing prayer team to "seek the greater gifts" that we might bear more fruit for Christ. Ask the Lord to expand His gifts in you. I have no doubt that the Lord gave me the gift of healing and will continue to pour out that gift as long as I continue to minister healing in His name. But I also pray for the other gifts as well. Bring it all on, Lord! I confess, with grateful joy in my heart, that I am surprised whenever I glimpse the evidence of other gifts in me. Please understand that I am boasting in the Lord, not in myself (2 Corinthians 10:17). I must, at all times, remain out of His way so that what is brought forth is Him, not me. As John the Baptist said, "He [Jesus] must increase, but I must decrease" (John 3:30 ESV). Make it so, dear Lord!

AUTHORITY

[Jesus] sent them out to proclaim the
kingdom of God and to heal the sick.
—Luke 9:2

For the first fifteen years of my healing ministry, I did not grasp the authority I had over disease and dis-ease. I'm not talking about "churchy" authority, as in hierarchy. I'm referring to the gentle, kind, compassionate authority that God has given to us in the gifts of the Holy Spirit over disease. You do not need to be an ordained minister, have a seminary degree, or be a member of the priesthood. You simply need to know what is at your disposal as a born-again, Spirit-filled follower of Christ. I want you to know that you are qualified to pray for healing too.

The authority that is available, is available simply because of our confident belief in Jesus, without doubt. When we believe Jesus Christ, then we know that when we pray to Him, He answers our prayers because His authority is in them. First John 5:14–15 confirms this: "This is the confidence we have in approaching God: that if we ask anything according to his will, he hears us. And if we know that he hears us—whatever we ask—we know that we have what we asked of him."

It may sound downright silly, but never having been told or never having studied authority (apart from my military experience), I was clueless about the authority that Christ vests in His faithful children. We are to take His authority over sickness and disease whenever we pray in faith and invoke Jesus' whole being and character. His authority is available to us because He gave it to us! Matthew 10:1 says: "Jesus called his twelve disciples to him and gave them authority to drive out impure spirits and to heal every disease and sickness."

Now that you know you have authority, take care not to abuse it. Praying for others is a sacred privilege, no matter how often you do it. I think of healing prayer as the times when I have held a person's soul in my hands for a short while.

Christ's authority is "accredited," but it cannot be bought. It is freely given, but we still have our part to do. We are accredited His authority when we demonstrate obedience to Him: "Therefore confess your sins to each other and pray for each other so that you may be healed. The prayer of a righteous person is powerful and effective" (James 5:16). Our authority in Christ is made evident in the power and effectiveness of our prayers. That power and effectiveness is born out of our obedience to Him, doing what He tells us to do and say. Jesus Himself modeled this for us by His own testimony in answering the Jewish leaders of the temple who challenged His authority: "Jesus gave them this answer: 'Very truly I tell you, the Son can do nothing by himself; he can do only what he sees his Father doing, because whatever the Father does the Son also does'" (John 5:19).

Indeed, Jesus was deliberate as He modeled absolute obedience to the Father for the benefit of His disciples and, ultimately, us. After His resurrection and ascension, Jesus sent His Holy Spirit to indwell His followers on earth. Those who have since been baptized in His Holy Spirit and acquainted with His ministry are also empowered to emulate His earthly conduct—doing only what the Father does and saying what the Father says. Just as Jesus confessed in John 5:19, we are to be like Him. We, too, can do nothing on our own accord but must do only what we see Him doing. We accomplish this when we fully rely upon His ongoing guidance through the indwelling of His Holy Spirit. Today, at this very moment, Christ's authority is rendered in you through the leading of His Holy Spirit. Through this perhaps new lens, please read and take to heart what Jesus told His disciples: "But the Advocate, the Holy Spirit, whom the Father will send in my name, will teach you all things and will remind you of everything I have said to you" (John 14:26).

Once we fully understand and believe we have Christ's authority and feel drawn to healing ministry, we must long to become as effective as possible. We want to be about our Father's business, recipients of His "Amen!" as we briefly hold the soul of a supplicant in the arms of our prayers. But here's the rub, and I need to be very clear here: one of the most important things we must do in this ministry is to get out of God's way. The more we do not try to pray in our own strength, the more palpably God is at work.

God always shows up—not because we are such fit prayer ministers but because He is supremely concerned about the welfare of the souls with whom He has entrusted us to pray. Sometimes He prompts us to stretch out our hands to heal others in very public places. If you are allowing the Holy Spirit to guide and direct you (not your aptitude to read faces, or your interpretation of words or actions, or your assumption about someone's tears), you will be privy to witnessing Him doing amazing things even in the most unlikely place. Very often, I have seen Him do this in the United States Post Office, where I have prayed for those in line, by the inspiration of His Spirit, and seen many set free of diseases. My post office branch has grown to accept my presence and actually loves when I visit! I do get a good deal of ribbing from the staff, however.

Prayer and God's gifts of healing and other gifts of His Spirit are all a mystery—a divine mystery. I have no formula for you to follow that will result in your becoming a more effective prayer minister. In truth, it is all about His love. In praying for healing, our intent is, with

His love, to help the supplicant to capture God's peace that passes all understanding. I believe that the environment Jesus creates during prayer is peace and love. During prayer we are instantly swept into a safe zone filled with the Holy Spirit, with Christ's love, and with certainty that our Lord is the same today as He was yesterday and will remain the same tomorrow. He commands us to be humble before Him when we pray for others.

That means that praying for others is never an EGO trip (Edging God Out). You are not elevated above others. You possess no power of your own, and there is no grandstanding allowed. When we stretch out our hands to pray for others, our very attitude and countenance must exhibit the same humility demonstrated by Jesus when He took upon Himself all our sins and went to the cross for our reconciliation with God. We all need to get that right.

So how can you become more effective in your prayers for others? How can you create and move into a safe zone, before God, with your supplicants? How can you get out of His way and allow Him to do the work through you? How can you really love someone into the healing presence of Jesus Christ?

As I have already stated, I have no formula. With the list below of ideas and measures we can use to become more effective prayer ministers, there is also no chronological or any other order, nor are some more important than others. I challenge you to begin with this list and work through each one. Meditate on them, pray into them, practice them, and add to them as you are led in the years ahead. This list is comprised of thoughts, words, and deeds that may help us draw closer to God by surrendering ourselves and aligning ourselves with His Word and His Spirit as we pray for others.

- *Settle your account with Jesus Christ.* Confess any sin you've tried to hide from Him. Address any doubt you may yet have. Have you surrendered your entire person, in body, mind, and spirit, to Him as your Savior? Have you submitted yourself completely to His lordship?

- *Ask Jesus for the infilling or indwelling or baptism of the Holy Spirit.* We read in John 1:33: "The man on whom you see the Spirit come down and remain is the one who will baptize with the Holy Spirit." And Mark 1:8 says: "I baptize you with [or "in"] water, but he [Jesus] will baptize you with [or "in"] the Holy Spirit."

- *Ask the Lord to give you all the gifts of the Holy Spirit as He deems necessary.* Ask Him to give His gifts of healing in particular. Search your Bible for all the passages listing the gifts of the Holy Spirit. Learn about them and ask Jesus for them.

- With the gifts of the Holy Spirit operating within you, be sure to *ask God to help you also manifest the fruits of the Spirit*, found in Galatians 5:22–23: "But the fruit of the Spirit is love, joy, peace, forbearance, kindness, goodness, faithfulness, gentleness and self-control." Meditate on those qualities and pray that you acquire all of them.

- *Study all the healing accounts of Jesus in the New Testament and all healing accounts in the Old Testament.* Search the word *heal* on Biblegateway.com.

- *Read as many books as you can on the subject of Christian healing, but read them with discernment.* Remember that the only official manual for Christian healing is the Bible and the only model for Christian healing is Jesus Christ. No matter which book you read or speaker you listen to, everything must line up with Jesus Christ and the Bible.

- *Be available as God's healing ambassador.* Whether you overhear someone express a need while at the grocery store, in the post office, or from your waiter at a restaurant, be bold. Offer: "How might I pray for you?"

- *Spend time meditating on 1 Corinthians 12:31: "Now eagerly* desire the greater gifts." Be sure to read this verse within the context of the whole chapter.

- *Meditate also on John 3:30:* "He must become greater; I must become less." Read it within the context of the chapter.
- *Identify the felt need and pray into that target,* seeing it in your mind's eye. Invade the expressed felt need with prayer, immersing the supplicant in love, peace, power, glory, and the perfect presence of the Lord Jesus.
- To better envision the need for which you have been asked to pray, *consider consulting, later, the internet or other resources in search of graphics or explanatory information that can help you intercede more effectively.*
- *Join a Christian healing community.* Seek out local churches or ministries that offer your community opportunities for healing prayer. See about getting a healing service started. Keep in mind that the official manual is the Bible and the only model is Jesus.
- *Vet local or regional ministries that offer healing prayer courses and workshops, and plan to attend.* Many offer online courses as well. It may be worth traveling to others.
- *Find a mentor or spiritual director.* Many Christian denominations have developed programs for spiritual direction. Find out if your pastor can recommend one to you.
- *Seek out prayer partners and accountability partners.* If you are drawn to healing ministry, you are called to community. There are no lone rangers in this ministry.
- Every time you pray for others, *you have been given a sacred trust.*
  - You are not to talk with others about those for whom you have prayed, unless they plan to harm themselves or others.
  - If you need guidance afterward (for example, from another prayer minister), do not reveal the identity of the supplicant. Share only what is utterly essential.
  - If you notice a friend or acquaintance has received prayer from

someone else, don't ask about the nature of the prayer they sought. Don't share with them or anyone—even your genuine concern. If they want you to know, they will tell you.

– When you have prayed for someone and see him or her the following week at church or at a store, never ask how they are doing. Do not dig up roots! Do not insinuate yourself in their lives—unless they initiate a discussion with you.

– Confidentiality is of the utmost importance. It's better to err on the side of silence, than ever to "out" your friend's, or any supplicant's, privacy.

- If you are praying within time constraints (for example, healing services, other church services, etc.), *try to have only one prayer minister pray aloud while the other intercedes silently.* Work out signals or keywords, beforehand, to use if the silent intercessor feels the Lord prompt them to add to the prayer.

- If you are scheduled to pray on a team and feel unwell— are wrestling with personal issues, lacking faith, or generally unfit—*find a replacement.* Do not force yourself.

- Before your team begins praying for others, *pray together for the Lord's protection, guidance, and provision for all.*

- When your team is done praying, at the end of the allotted prayer time, *pray with thanksgiving* for the Lord's provision and for your release from any strongholds.

- *Do not give advice, under any circumstances, when praying for supplicants.* No doctor referrals, medicine ideas, coping skills, psych analyses—*no advice!*

- If praying for someone who has deeper needs beyond the allotted time, don't dive into healing of memories, inner healing, or extended prayer, which should be reserved for private appointments. At the end tell supplicants of other available services should they desire a private appointment. Do not tell them what they need. *Simply offer follow-up information.*

- *Come alongside supplicants.* Picture in your mind being shoulder to shoulder with them. Healing prayer is best offered "with" supplicants, not "to" or "for" them.
- If praying as teams during a church or healing service, be sure to:
  - Tell the supplicant your first names.
  - Ask the supplicant their first name and inquire, "How might we pray for you?"
  - Ask permission to touch them (appropriately) during the "laying on of hands." Some supplicants may have hidden issues and do not want to be touched. If it is permissible, then lightly touch their head, shoulder, arm, or back.
- *Never lord it over others—neither supplicants nor prayer partners.* No controlling spirits, no bossy stuff. Check yourself for disingenuous "spiritual" voices or manifestations.
- *If you are out of your depth, refer.* Talk to your clergy. You are not alone.
- *Do not limit God.* Don't get in His way. He will do what He will do. Just let Him do it!
- *Have a teachable spirit.* Be open to suggestions that could increase your effectiveness.
- *Be a Barnabas,* who accompanied Paul on many missions. He was an encourager, and so can you be also. Ask the Lord to anoint you with this gift of His Holy Spirit.
- *Put on the mind and compassion of Christ.* Healing ministry requires that we know our Lord Jesus in every way as we put on His mind and minister in His Spirit as we pray.
- If you are drawn to healing ministry, you are called to learn and grow deeper in Him. You will always be a "learner." Just as you give prayer freely, *seek prayer freely* as well.
- *Meditate on Ephesians 3:20–21:* "Now to him who is able to do immeasurably more than all we ask or imagine, according to his power that is at work within us, to him be glory in the

church and in Christ Jesus throughout all generations, for ever and ever! Amen."

- *Pray more.* Pray while driving, working, or playing. Pray alone or with others. Pray for others. Pray to receive and pray to be privileged to give. Pray aloud or silently. Just pray!

Though the list above is long and may appear exhaustive, it is not. There is so much more that the Lord will show you in your endeavor to offer healing prayer to those in need. Jesus will both add to this list and help you edit yourself whenever you stretch out your hand to pray in His name. Every time you pray for the healing of others, you also are being healed. It is the most glorious adventure, and those drawn to it never stop discovering new facets of the person of our Lord and Savior, Jesus Christ.

It has been a long time since 1990, when I first stretched out my hand to pray for a woman customer at my frame shop in Connecticut. Every supplicant since has introduced a new situation, helped me with a new understanding, and offered something fresh to contemplate. This will never end. I am a perpetual student—delighting in the glorious opportunity to see our God move in and among His children.

Becoming a more effective prayer minister is all about intent. What is your intention? Do you desire to be noticed and loved—or is it your intention to simply serve Christ in humility as you listen, love, and pray for His children? I pray it is always the latter. Should you ever suspect that the former is in operation, you will need to lay it down until He restores you, in His time, to this ministry. This is never a right; it is a privilege—and one to be done in obedience to Jesus Christ!

ARMOR OF GOD

Therefore put on the full armor of God, so
that when the day of evil comes, you may
be able to stand your ground, and after
you have done everything, to stand.
—EPHESIANS 6:13

Paul weaponized God's Word in Ephesians 6. Using the body armor of a Roman soldier, Paul outlined a tough defense against our enemy, the Devil, who prowls around ready to devour us. Paul detailed the apparel worn by military combatants of his day to protect themselves. He used the kitted-out Roman soldier as a metaphor in his letter to the Ephesians, much as Jesus used parables to teach us as recorded in the Gospels. Here is the Ephesians 6:10–17 passage in its entirety:

Finally, be strong in the Lord and in his mighty power. Put on the full armor of God, so that you can take your stand against the devil's schemes. For our struggle is not against flesh and blood, but against the rulers, against the authorities, against the powers of this dark world and against the spiritual forces of evil in the heavenly realms. Therefore put on the full armor of God, so that when the day of evil comes, you may be able to stand your ground, and after you have done everything, to stand. Stand firm then, with the belt of truth buckled around your waist, with the breastplate of righteousness in place, and with your feet fitted with the readiness that comes from the gospel of peace. In addition to all this, take up the shield of faith, with which you can extinguish all the flaming arrows of the evil one. Take the helmet of salvation and the sword of the Spirit, which is the word of God.

Wow! The girdle of truth, the breastplate of righteousness, the shoes of peace, the helmet of salvation, the shield of faith, and the sword of the Spirit . . . everything necessary for our protection and equipment in a healing ministry as soldiers for Christ! Paul was fore-warning us that there is a battle going on whether we can see it or not. This battle is against powers and principalities, not against people who stand before us. "For our struggle is not against flesh and blood, but against the rulers, against the authorities, against the powers of this dark world and against the spiritual forces of evil in the heavenly realms" (v. 12).

We who minister in healing must be aware that God has called and commissioned us to His frontlines. Regardless of how "tame" things may appear on the surface of the ministry of healing, the enemy of our souls is hard at work to corrupt God's good Creation. Sickness, disease, injury, and all manner of evil are the result of the work of the Devil. These perils are the Devil's assault upon Creation, and our God wants His children equipped to be victorious over the evil one. We who seek healing for ourselves, or on behalf of others, must never forget 1 John 4:4: "You, dear children, are from God and have overcome them, because the one who is in you is greater than the one who is in the world."

Now please pair 1 John 4:4 with these verses from Paul's letter to the Romans. We must not be spooked or distracted by the enemy's tactics! Amen?

What, then, shall we say in response to these things? If God is for us, who can be against us? (Romans 8:31)

No, in all these things we are more than conquerors through him who loved us. For I am convinced that neither death nor life, neither angels nor demons, neither the present nor the future, nor any powers, neither height nor depth, nor anything else in all creation, will be able to separate us from the love of God that is in Christ Jesus our Lord. (Romans 8:37–39)

Indeed, it is the Lord who calls us to ministry and the Lord who provides for us to accomplish His assignment. As we read in Hebrews, Jesus equips us for the ministry to which He calls us.

Now may the God of peace, who through the blood of the eternal covenant brought back from the dead our Lord Jesus, that great Shepherd of the sheep, equip you with everything good for doing his will, and may he work in us what is pleasing to him, through Jesus Christ, to whom be glory for ever and ever. Amen. (Hebrews 13:20–21)

When I think of the full armor of God, it brings to mind images of the Crusaders' warrior garb worn by the knights on their military missions. The Crusades began about 1095 and continued on, in some form or other, until 1492. Many orders of the Crusades wore the familiar red cross on their breastplates or shields. Legend has it that British knights of yore would spend twenty-four hours in the castle's oratory or chapel, either wearing their armor or placing it near the altar as they knelt in prayer vigil before God for His protection. Today, the armor worn by our military is either flak jackets or body armor. We are so grateful to military chaplains who still pray for our servicemen and -women before, during, and after they engage in combat.

So, if God has instructed us to fight the good fight for His name's sake, then we must be certain to gear up and prepare for battle against the enemy every day. Though we do not physically put on these items, we envision ourselves donning these protective items, while we pray before our King, in preparation for engaging the adversity in our world. Our gear—the girdle, the breastplate, the shoes, the helmet, the shield, and the sword—are necessary for us to be "dressed" for combat. Only then are we equipped and prepared to do battle for the good health and salvation of those who come for healing of their hearts, minds, bodies, and souls.

This all may sound rather warlike and too aggressive, but as healing prayer ministers we are called to the front lines to defend against diseases. If we are to be victorious over sickness that the Devil has initiated, we must confront the diagnoses, the ill effects of treatment, the physical pain, and the emotional wounds that supplicants struggle with as they seek healing. What I have heard during these past thirty years could have left me flat on my back and despairing, were it not for the whole armor of God to protect me. Many stories, told to me by supplicants, are so vile that I have difficulty imagining how they manage to get out of bed each morning. Though I sit across from a person who looks perfectly normal on the outside, I know that person has invisible gaping wounds and emotional scar tissue on his or her insides—a veritable oozing mass of toxic hurting.

Without following the instructions found in the Ephesians 6 passage, I am not certain that I could face the challenges of each day. I pray into the whole armor of God before my day begins. Doing so reminds me that my faith is grounded in the person of Jesus Christ and His great and precious promises. Sometimes I have prayed that the breastplate of righteousness will be so shining that the light of Christ will penetrate the darkness of the lives of those who are defeated and hopeless.

Praying that the helmet of salvation would protect our heads, minds, and eyes brings me enormous peace. The helmets of Roman soldiers had visors, which is what I envision as I pray. A time-honored tradition for soldiers, equipped with visors, was to lift the visor up with an unarmed right hand to reveal the identity of the person behind the visor. This act eventually birthed the modern salute we are familiar with today. The British soldier salutes by raising a flat palm to the forehead out of respect, while the American military salute displays a hand tilted forward, indicating that the one saluting could be armed.

There are fewer than forty references to armor in the Bible. Most of them are found in the Old Testament. Of the five in the New Testament, however, three are in Ephesians 6. Paul's letter is a warning shot that this armor business is serious stuff. He is implying that we are not to lie around on our laurels and expect healing to readily come our way. The enemy, who is the instigator of evil, is like a devouring lion and has much to lose when Christians confront him with God's power and might. Paul is saying that the full armor is another of Christ's gifts, tailor-made for us. However, we must *open* our gift and not just talk about it admiringly. He wants us to don that armor daily. Though it won't ever wear out, we will surely be worn out if we fail to use it.

I noted, upon reading the Ephesians 6:10–17 passage again, that it is both defensive and offensive in its strategy. Yes, the passage is primarily defensive, calling us to stand firm, have our feet fitted with the gospel of peace, and extinguish the flaming arrows of the evil one—until verse 11, which says, "Put on the full armor of God, so that you can take your stand against the devil's schemes." It is an offensive stand. It is reminiscent of the adage "The best defense is a good offense," an axiom that is applied to many endeavors, including sports and military maneuvers. Wikipedia calls this the "strategic offensive principle of war." God is brilliant, isn't He?

In defending our ground, we are also taking ground from our enemy. In the healing ministry, it is crystal clear that when we pray for a disease or wound to be gone, we are taking the ground back from the enemy! Whenever captives of sickness and emotional wounding are set free to live in the fullness of Christ, we have reclaimed the ground for our God.

In the midst of all this combative jargon, however, it is easy to overlook what is arguably the most important "article" of the whole armor of God as found in Ephesians 6:10–17; that is, we are not finished putting on the whole armor until we have accomplished verse 18: "And pray in the Spirit on all occasions with all kinds of prayers and requests. With this in mind, be alert and always keep on praying for all the Lord's people." The full armor of Ephesians 6 is not complete until we take stock of God's command that we pray in the Spirit on all occasions with all kinds of prayers and requests.

God is with us, always ready to strengthen, defend, and preserve His creation. Our job is to be willing to go whenever He sends us, wherever He sends us, equipped with every gift He has provided to overcome whatever evil His children encounter. In our case, as healing prayer ministers, we are called to stand in complete confidence and doubtless faith that Jesus Christ is able and willing to heal anyone who will place his trust in Him.

For a year of my life during the 1970s, while serving in Her Majesty's Royal Marines in Ireland, I wore body armor. Our armor was from America, used and left over from Vietnam. There was always something comforting about putting it on, giving me a sense of protection. The armor we wore was bulky, heavy, and smelled nasty whenever it rained. It took a while to get used to wearing it, but then it became second nature. Putting on that flak jacket was a stark reminder that we were going into battle, about to engage in combat with an enemy who wanted us dead.

In all honesty, dear souls, the armor God is asking us to wear every day serves the same purpose as the armor I wore in Ireland. As Christian soldiers we will daily engage in battle with an enemy that God warns us, again and again, wants us dead. Listen to Him and follow His instructions. He loves you and He wants you to be safe and victorious!

As soon as I am awake in the morning, I smile and put on the whole armor of God. Then I claim the blood of Christ to wash over me and protect me. I have added an adapted version of the beautiful Prayer of St. Patrick to my daily preparation:

Christ before me, Christ behind me, Christ to the left of me, Christ to the right of me, Christ above me, Christ below me, Christ within me, Christ to win me. Amen.

Then, I am ready . . . equipped for whatever ministry He calls me to that day, able to withstand the fiery darts that may come in my direction.

I do not mean to aggrandize my preparation and adherence to His instructions; I only want to affirm that His likening of our doing ministry to engaging in combat is not tongue in cheek. He knows better than any of us what we are facing. He is omniscient, omnipotent, and omnipresent. Like the Roman centurion who sought Jesus to heal his ailing servant, I understand authority (Matthew 8:7–9). I yield to Christ's authority and endeavor to follow His mandates with precision.

What then are we promised when we adhere to His admonitions? *This*, as found in Isaiah 58:8–9:

> Then your light will break forth like the dawn,
> and your healing will quickly appear;
> then your righteousness will go before you,
> and the glory of the LORD will be your rear guard.
> Then you will call, and the LORD will answer;
> you will cry for help, and he will say: Here am I.

The Lord, our God, is a shield about us. He is our glory and the lifter of our heads. He will protect us and we will stand firm in our confident faith in Him, for we know that "the LORD will go before you, the God of Israel will be your rear guard" (Isaiah 52:12) and "the glory of the LORD will be your rear guard" (Isaiah 58:8).

My mug, when I was young lad, was a rather splendid container for my "cuppa" (cup of) tea. It was gold trimmed with a painting of a youth catching a fish. The quote on it said: "Lord grant that I may catch a fish so big that even I, when speaking of it afterwards, may have no need to lie."

As you apply these truths to the ministry of distributing Christ's healing gifts, you will see and hear miracles that your eye has never before seen nor your ear has ever before heard. Never forget that all healing is done by God, only. You and I, in making ourselves available as His humble servants, are but vessels through whom He is glorified.

Go in peace, equipped to love and serve the Lord! Alleluia!

COURAGE

This is the confidence we have in approaching God: that
if we ask anything according to his will, he hears us.
—1 JOHN 5:14

It takes courage to be a prayer minister. It takes courage to ask someone those six small but powerful words, "How may I pray for you?" If there is fear in asking, it is perhaps because there is fear of being rejected. Frankly, I know of no one who in some manner has not been rejected upon asking those words. Sometimes healing prayer ministers are erroneously perceived as hocus-pocus "faith healers." In Christian healing ministry there is only one valid source of faith invoked in prayer; that is, the faith of the prayer minister(s) in God's ability to heal. Some supplicants flat out refuse prayer because of their misperceptions of the prayer minister based on appearance, gender, voice, or demeanor.

It takes courage for prayer ministers to step out of their comfort zones and publicly demonstrate their faith in God's desire and ability to heal those in need. To volunteer to stand in the gap between a sick person and God Almighty takes an unflinching willingness to be vulnerable. Only those emboldened by the Holy Spirit will stand in that gap without doubt and stretch out their hands in the name of Jesus Christ to heal those willing to receive His healing gifts.

Many writers have dealt with courage, but in my research for this book, I found a brilliant book by W. Ryan Rebold called *Nothing but Faith in My Pocket*. The chapter "Fear Leads to Failure" includes the following quote, worth sharing here:

Here's a lion chaser's manifesto: Quit living as if the purpose of life is to arrive safely at death. Grab life by the mane. Set God-sized goals. Pursue God-ordained passions. Go after a dream that is destined to fail without divine intervention. Keep asking questions. Keep making mistakes. Keep seeking God. Stop pointing out problems and become part of the solution. Stop repeating the past and start creating the future. Stop playing it safe and start taking risks. Expand your horizons. Accumulate experiences. Consider the lilies. Enjoy the journey. Find every excuse you can to celebrate everything you can. Live like today is the first and last day of your life. Don't let what's wrong with you keep you from worshiping what's right with God. Burn sinful bridges. Blaze a new trail. Criticize by creating. Worry less about what people think and more about what God thinks. Don't try to be who you are not. Be yourself. Laugh at yourself. Quit holding out. Quit holding back. Quit running away.[1]

Now do us both a favor and reread the sentence from the above quote wherein I will now take the liberty to replace the word *dream* with "call to ministry": "Go after a [call to ministry] that is destined to fail without divine intervention." When we stall out or become stymied in responding to any call to ministry, it is always due to a lack of courage. Our faith may have been weak at the time or our circumstances difficult, but in hindsight we will identify a lack of courage. God wants us to believe Him—even in the face of what appear to be insuperable obstacles.

As for that bit about "living as if the purpose of life is to arrive safely at death," be advised that healing prayer ministers are never called to play it safe. Our call is not compatible with simply biding time, treading water, standing still, retreating, or hiding out until death delivers us. God's call to prayer ministry must rely upon God alone—not on intelligence, personality, connections, or group thinking. Prayer ministers cannot be trained. They are called by God, taught by His Word, and guided by His Holy Spirit. Otherwise, as Rebold poignantly pointed out, we are "destined to fail"!

As I write this, I feel my former drill instructor self welling up within me and wanting to shout out words of encouragement here: "Come on lads, you can do this!"

Whenever I speak to groups and include a talk on courage, I usually inquire, "How many here have seen *The Wizard of Oz*?" I am always amazed at the number of folks who claim to have watched it more than thirty times. Whenever I think of this movie, what comes to mind is the dream sequence. Remember? The tin man wanted a heart. The scarecrow wanted a brain, and the lion wanted courage. Listen with me to the lion now: "Put 'em up, put 'em up, I'll fight you with one arm behind my back. Oh, I scare myself sometimes." Then he bursts into song. "If I were the king of the forest, not a queen, not a duke, not a prince, my real robes of the forest . . ." I just watched it again on YouTube![2]

One Sunday I visited a church where the rector asked me to pray for his entire congregation, one at a time! To accommodate his request, I asked the parishioners to simply tell me one word that expressed their prayer request (grandmother, cancer, sick cat, and so forth). It was going rather well until a seven-year-old stood rigid before me, unable to speak. I was instantly reminded of my traumatic boarding school days when I would freeze every time the teacher called upon me to answer a question. I tried to help this young lad by suggesting some possible prayer needs he might have: "Is everything okay with your siblings?"

"It's not that," he replied indignantly.

"Well," I countered, "how about your homework?"

The child cut me off and replied, "It's not that either."

I persisted with more suggestions but could not engage him. Soon I noticed that his eyes were trained straight ahead, just beyond me, almost trance-like. As he gazed at the stained-glass window behind me and over the altar, an angelic look came over his face and at long last he broke his silence. "I know," he whispered, his voice gaining boldness, "I know what I want . . . I want wisdom." His words stopped me in my tracks. This seven-year-old child had asked for wisdom! I thought to myself that if he could ask for wisdom, I would do the same for myself. Since then I have faithfully incorporated into my prayer life requests for courage and wisdom.

Regrettably, I have met too many people who would not dare whisper a request for wisdom or courage, much less pray for them. Their greatest fear is the fear of failure. They often begin a project and, inevitably, shoot themselves in the foot, hijacking their success and calling it quits prematurely. Their fear of success is so overpowering that they would do just about anything to ensure they do not succeed. The only way we can overcome this kind of fear is to confront it—and that requires courage.

Courage is running toward the lion's roar, not hiding from the lions prowling about.

As a former Royal Marine drill instructor, I witnessed many recruits who greatly feared navigating a submerged tunnel challenge on the mandatory endurance course. In their efforts to earn their famed green berets, Royal Marine recruits are plunged, horizontally, face down in black, murky water and are expected to safely make their way through a dark, entirely submerged, very narrow tunnel. One marine is assigned to push recruits into the tunnel entrance, and another must grab anything he can to pull recruits out of it, one by one. If either marine on duty, responsible for pushing or pulling, fails to do his job correctly, a recruit could very well drown. Indeed, deaths have occurred in the tunnel, as it is too constricted for the recruits to use their arms to swim out.

The recruits must trust someone else with their very lives. It's not the best feeling in the world having to rely on your "oppos" ("friends" in Royal Marine slang). Sadly, some recruits bail out of all further training because of this challenge, refusing to even try to complete it. When we lack the courage to trust and believe Jesus, we are like the recruits who are unable to entrust their mates with their lives. Similarly, it can take courage to entrust a prayer minister, who is often a stranger, to pray for our healing.

It is Paul who wrote these familiar words in Philippians 4:13, "I can do everything through Christ, who gives me strength" (NLT). Now, I ask, do you remember the verse that follows these words? When I speak to groups, I often ask that same question. Only once has someone known! I was speaking at a Roman Catholic parish when a woman delightedly responded that she knew the answer (though she later confessed that her Bible happened to be open to that very verse). The next verse is so very powerful: "Yet it was good of you to share in my troubles" (v. 14).

Paul, who is often referred to as the "grandfather of the church," wrote those words. In verse 13, Paul was sharing how very reliably we can count on Jesus; but in verse 14, he is also publishing his gratitude for fellow believers, upon whom he relied to help carry his burdens. We, who believe in Jesus Christ, are to courageously trust our fellow brothers and sisters to bear our burdens. If only all Royal Marines recruits believed Jesus, all might well achieve their green berets.

Is it fear holding you back from living life in abundance? If we wait to do something until we are certain it's right, we probably will never get much done. It is courage that we need in order to bridge the chasm caused by fear. Do you need an infilling of courage to embolden you to get off the starting block? F.E.A.R. is an acronym for: False Evidence Appearing Real. Consider that fear is often a trick that the enemy of our souls uses to keep us off our game and unable to succeed. We must remind ourselves that our enemy instills fear within us by fabricating false evidence that appears real and is designed to keep us immobilized. Fear knocked on the door; faith answered and there was no one there.

Courageous Steps for Fear-Filled Folk

It takes courage to
say "sorry."
say "I forgive you."

say "I love you."

say "I believe Jesus."

say "I love You, Jesus."

go to a doctor.

trust doctors.

ask for prayer.

make decisions.

stand on the promises of God.

say "I need courage."

ask for help.

trust those who help you.

say yes to God.

say no to friends and family.

live life in abundance and not in scarcity.

walk away from abuse.

set healthy boundaries.

resist gossip.

press through pain.

walk through the valley of the shadow of death.

overcome your fears.

pray for the sick.

trust Jesus to heal.

follow Jesus Christ.

move from being "victim" to becoming "victor."

It takes courage to live.

Here is the wisdom of biblical passages regarding courage:

But blessed is the one who trusts in the LORD, whose confidence is in him. They will be like a tree planted by the water that sends out its roots by the stream. It does not fear when heat comes; its leaves are always green. It has no worries in a year of drought and never fails to bear fruit. (Jeremiah 17:7–8)

This passage from Jeremiah resonates with a modern saying heard so often in our daily lives: "no worries." I can almost hear it said with an Aussie accent as I write.

It is God who arms me with strength and keeps my way secure. (Psalm 18:32)

So, we say with confidence, "The Lord is my helper; I will not be afraid. What can mere mortals do to me?" (Hebrews 13:6)

Be on your guard; stand firm in the faith; be courageous; be strong. Do everything in love. (1 Corinthians 16:13–14)

So do not throw away your confidence; it will be richly rewarded. (Hebrews 10:35)

Be strong and courageous. Do not be afraid or terrified because of them, for the LORD your God goes with you; he will never leave you nor forsake you. (Deuteronomy 31:6)

For God has not given us a spirit of fear, but of power and of love and of a sound mind. (2 Timothy 1:7 NKJV)

Perhaps my favorite verses on courage are Isaiah 35:3–4 as found in *The Message*:

> Energize the limp hands,
> strengthen the rubbery knees.
> Tell fearful souls,
> "Courage! Take heart!
> God is here, right here,
> on his way to put things right

And redress all wrongs.
He's on his way! He'll save you!"

The unclean woman in Matthew 9 so believed Jesus for her healing that she boldly stretched out her hand, risking harsh retribution from those gathered, and dared to touch Jesus as He passed by:

> Just then a woman who had been subject to bleeding for twelve years came up behind him and touched the edge of his cloak. She said to herself, "If I only touch his cloak, I will be healed." Jesus turned and saw her. "Take heart, daughter," he said, "your faith has healed you." And the woman was healed at that moment. (Matthew 9:20–22)

It also took courage for Joseph to ask Pilate for Jesus' dead body to be taken off the cross in Mark 15:43: "Joseph of Arimathea, a prominent member of the Council, who was himself waiting for the kingdom of God, went boldly to Pilate and asked for Jesus' body."

And even Jesus sought courage to complete His earthly mission: "When it came close to the time for his Ascension, he gathered up his courage and steeled himself for the journey to Jerusalem" (Luke 9:51 THE MESSAGE).

The first of two pivotal Bible passages that identify the foundation of our courage as being Jesus, is found in 1 John 5:14–15: "This is the confidence we have in approaching God: that if we ask anything according to his will, he hears us. And if we know that he hears us—whatever we ask—we know that we have what we asked of him." And the second is from Hebrews 4:15–16: "For we do not have a high priest who is unable to empathize with our weaknesses, but we have one who has been tempted in every way, just as we are—yet he did not sin. Let us then approach God's throne of grace with confidence, so that we may receive mercy and find grace to help us in our time of need."

Dear friends, the above verses assure us that confident faith in Jesus Christ guarantees an outpouring of His courage whenever we have need. Do not overlook these verses. Do not overanalyze them either, for they unequivocally tell us that our Lord and Savior meant it when He declared on the cross that "It is finished!" He does not waffle on His promises. Though He appeared in the image of man, Jesus never suffered the sinful flaws of human character. His Word is His bond. He is the same today as He was yesterday and will be tomorrow!

I implore you to stop beating up on yourself and to get on with the business of living. No matter what our circumstances, nothing is out of Christ's control when we surrender ourselves to Him. Never forget these precious words penned by St. Paul in his letter to the Romans: "Therefore, there is now no condemnation for those who are in Christ Jesus" (8:1). And now having been apprised of all these passages, let us live them out in and through Christ. Gather up your courage, stand firm in your faith in Jesus Christ, and surrender every fear to Jesus. He will neither leave you nor forsake you. Just as turtles cannot make forward progress without sticking their necks out, so must we. But we are *not* to go it alone. Let's ask Jesus to be our GPS and equip us with His confidence and courage en route!

Jesus said, "Take courage! It is I. Don't be afraid" (Matthew 14:27).

Take courage, dear soul. You really can do this.

LISTEN, LOVE,
AND PRAY

He must become greater; I must become less.
—John 3:30

In 2003 I was called to lead the Healing Ministry of the Episcopal Diocese of Albany, New York, located at the Christ the King Spiritual Life Center in Greenwich, New York. After about a month in the office, so many things were happening. As a layperson at the time, I was unsure of my boundaries. Recalling the wisdom of Hebrews 13:7–8—"Remember your leaders, who spoke the word of God to you. Consider the outcome of their way of life and imitate their faith. Jesus Christ is the same yesterday and today and forever"—I called the suffragan bishop, the Rt. Rev. David Bena, and confessed to him that I was totally out of my depth.

"Bishop Dave, what are my boundaries?" I asked. He responded with words I shall never forget: "Nigel, I trust you. I trust the Holy Spirit, so get on with it!" Well, I was given my orders in a very godly fashion, so I simply obeyed and got on with the "business" of healing—God's business of healing.

As we discussed in chapter 3, as a born-again believer in Christ you already have at your disposal the gentle, kind, compassionate authority

God has given to us in the gifts of the Holy Spirit over disease. It is available because of our confident belief in Jesus, and when we pray to Him, He answers our prayers because His authority is in them. If you never abuse it, taking care to listen, love, and pray when you have the opportunity to pray for a supplicant's healing, then you may very well be called to the healing ministry. I find that those called to healing prayer ministry possess these additional and primary attributes.

Listen

To have the gift of listening to others is truly remarkable. Sometimes it seems that people have stopped listening. Take this idea for a test drive the next time you are engaged in listening to someone: ask yourself how much time you actually listened and how much time you spent formulating your response. Is the time you spent formulating a response really listening? I think not.

When you are truly listening, you will also pay attention to body language. Much is communicated to us nonverbally when we are engaged in conversation. When you speak, be conscious of not only the words that come out of your mouth but also your body language. Square off with those you are engaged with and look at them. Eye contact is critical to genuine listening. When you look a person in the eye as you listen or speak to them, both parties feel "heard." Too often people speak while distractedly looking around. Instead, you might try to lock eyes with the person you are listening or speaking to, indicating that you don't want to miss anything.

Spend time observing others' conversations. Watch the body language of the people engaged. How much are they saying with words and how much with body language? As you undertake this exercise, I do want to share this caveat. Just as the same words can mean different things to different people, so can body language. I am sure we all have met someone who always smiles or grins while speaking. They can deliver the most devastating news with a smile on their face, which completely contradicts their words! So while you should pay close attention, take care to assess the whole picture, not just snippets based on your preset interpretations of others' words and actions.

During prayer sessions, I listen intently with my ears and my eyes. As you listen, it is helpful to feed back snippets in the supplicant's own words, indicating what you heard them say (for example, "Ah, he called you twice" or "Of course, you had no reason to doubt him"). This reassures the person that you are paying attention. Try also interjecting confirming words like, "I understand." "Yes, of course." "I see." It is also important to feed back details that you want to be sure you've grasped correctly (for example, "Help me understand . . . he died when you were twelve years old, leaving behind you, your brothers, and your grandmother to care for you"). Active listening techniques in conversation can help to express patience and compassion to supplicants.

Bite your tongue whenever you are tempted to compare scar tissue, injuries, or illnesses. Even if you had the same surgery last week, do not share your information as it will sound dismissive and will usually derail the supplicant's story. Even saying, "I had that operation. It was a painful recovery, but I made it and I'm sure you will too" is not only condescending but shifts the conversation to you. When you have invited a supplicant to share their story with you, you must listen, actively and affirmatively. It is *not* about you! Pay close attention to all the supplicant is saying, making mental note of what they are not saying, and listening intently to what God is saying. Oftentimes, I grab my chin or rest my hand across my mouth to indicate I am listening closely and to reduce any temptation to interrupt them.

Some people's stories are truly horrific, and you may find yourself shedding a tear. That is normal! Remember we are to "Rejoice with those who rejoice, weep with those who weep" (Romans 12:15 RSV). But please do not fall apart! If you see that a supplicant's story is triggering a place of palpable pain in your own life, surreptitiously excuse yourself, leaving the supplicant with your prayer partner, and return when you are calm. Showing compassion is truly a great gift— but it must be in moderation. Great displays of emotion may not only derail the supplicant's story but could jeopardize their ripeness for healing.

Jesus wept. And, yes, we were designed to cry. However, displays of heightened emotion can easily shift the focus from the supplicant's needs to *your* needs.

Listen with all your heart, with all your mind, with all your body, and with all your soul.

Love

God is love! "Whoever does not love does not know God, because God is love" (1 John 4:8).

A felonious child pornographer was sent by court order to meet with a healing minister in Florida. Having served his prison time, he was released but was required to seek ongoing treatment options, which included Christian healing ministry. My friend, the healing minister, knew this man was on her calendar. She was a mother, and no matter how she prayed, she rued this appointment. So preoccupied was she that she got a speeding ticket en route to meet him.

As she dragged herself up the stairs to her prayer room, where she was told the man was waiting, she protested under her breath, "Lord, I can't do this!" God answered loud and clear, "Since when has this ministry ever relied upon *you*?" "But . . . ," she retorted. "No 'buts,'" He boomed back at her. "Trust Me. Just get out of My way!"

She said it was really rough going for the first ten minutes. The man was defensive, combative, and aggressive. He told her vile things. She prayed silently in tongues, in her spiritual prayer language, as she listened to him. Years ago, raising children and forced to shorten her prayer times, she'd discovered that her Spirit could pray while her mind was otherwise engaged. Then she spied a beam of light briefly target him through an adjacent window and his face shone, just long enough for her to see him through God's eyes. In that instant, she was flooded with God's love and compassion for the precious soul of this broken person.

Read with me this passage from St. Paul's letter to the Romans, and open your eyes to see that absolutely nothing can separate us from God's love—unless, of course, *we* want to separate ourselves: "For I am convinced that neither death nor life, neither angels nor demons, neither the present nor the future, nor any powers, neither height nor depth, nor anything else in all creation, will be able to separate us from the love of God that is in Christ Jesus our Lord" (8:38–39).

Many years ago, a supplicant told me a story that caused me to become suddenly and violently nauseous. It would not be appropriate to tell you the story. I had to quickly leave the prayer room and deal with it. After a trip to the restroom, I stood in the corridor, outside the prayer room I had vacated, wrestling with God: "I don't want to go back into that room, Lord." So present is He, always, especially when we are in the midst of serving Him, that I was instantly filled with His divine peace. It truly did surpass all understanding. It was as though the Lord was saying to me, "Nigel, get back in that room and find something in that person to love." I went back inside and was able to do just that. Somehow, I pressed through the nausea and came to love the soul who was sitting in front of me. Supernaturally, I was able to focus on the love of Jesus for this person.

You also will have moments like these, for sure. Some prayer ministers may encounter a supplicant that is rather disagreeable, while others may confront pure evil. No matter what, look for God to show you something to love in the person God has placed in front of you. Prevailing through bad breath, body odor, a nasty disposition, or an unmitigated tale of evil, find whatever is loveable about that soul in God's eyes. No, he or she may not be lovely—but trust God that the person is worthy of His love.

At times like these, it is good to remember the greatest commandment found in Matthew 22:37–39: "'Love the Lord your God with all your heart and with all your soul and with all your mind.' This is the first and greatest commandment. And the second is like it: 'Love your neighbor as yourself.'" I would be remiss not to point out that the "second" commandment quoted here requires something that may yet be lacking in you, much less in those you'll be called to pray for. You must love yourself. If you do not love yourself, you cannot love your neighbor. Chew on that awhile, and if you continue to resist truly loving yourself, seek healing prayer to overcome this block to healing in you, before engaging in any meaningful way in healing prayer for others.

My prayer is that you will not feel called to healing ministry until you have discovered how to find something to love in every person you meet, including yourself. If you learn to live like this, your life will be changed forever.

> Now these three remain: faith, hope and love. But the greatest of these is love. (1 Corinthians 13:13)

Pray

We have arrived at the crux of the process healing ministers must follow: listen, love, and pray. It is as though the first two are preparation for the third, for without listening to a supplicant's story and without having God's love for them, healing prayers bounce off the ceiling, never reaching His throne of grace. Beloved, to pray effectively and with His power, we must know Jesus Christ.

First Corinthians 2:16 tells us, "But we have the mind of Christ."

To engage in healing prayer, we simply must be in Christ. Our faith and confidence in Him and His healing gifts must be complete and without doubt. If you were able to read the previous sections on listening and loving without flinching about your call, this section, "Pray," could confront your weakness.

Yes, indeed, we do have the mind of Christ when we are buried in Him, born again in Him, and baptized in His Holy Spirit. Being buried, born again, and baptized, we will hear Him speak and guide us as He entrusts His hurting children for us to intercede on their behalves in prayer. Second Corinthians 10:5 suggests how we can clear away any cobwebs that may obscure our confident faith in Him: "We demolish arguments and every pretension that sets itself up against the knowledge of God, and we take captive every thought to make it obedient to Christ."

Is there anything lacking in our faith? If there is any block in our belief that Jesus is truly who He claims to be, then we must petition Him, just as the father of the convulsing son, tormented by an unclean spirit since birth, modeled for us (Mark 9). Mind you, that father had tempered his request by saying to Jesus, "If you can do anything, take pity on us and help us" (v. 22). Jesus, a bit put off by the father's words "if you can," corrected him, saying, "Everything is possible for one who believes" (v. 23). Upon hearing that, "immediately the boy's father exclaimed, 'I do believe; help me overcome my unbelief!'" (v. 24).

God is so faithful that even when we are weak in our faith, we can confess that we do believe while asking Him to help us overcome our unbelief. Prayer ministers who encounter major, horrific illnesses in those for whom they pray, can be confronted with a similar "lack of belief." God's faithful prayer ministers who know how to listen, love, and pray know that He can heal their unbelief if they ask Him. Indeed, He will even help you take captive every thought that impedes your faith and will make those thoughts obedient to Him!

You see, prayer ministers are called to pray in faith: on behalf of

Christ, in Christ, and with Christ. All effective and powerful prayers are His, not ours. It is not about you and me! Are you getting this? He prays through us if we will yield to Him. He will give us the words when we pray, because He knows best what our supplicant needs and loves him or her more than anyone else ever will.

Read this: "And when you pray, do not keep on babbling like pagans, for they think they will be heard because of their many words" (Matthew 6:7). This would almost be humorous if it weren't so true—"babbling like pagans." Oh, dear! Let's be sure to avoid giving supplicants "their money's worth" by praying with far too many words. Allow Jesus to give us His words to pray.

I take the act of praying for supplicants very seriously. It is such a privilege to be allowed by God to see Him touch souls when we pray as He directs. When I pray for someone, I often imagine his or her soul sitting in the palm of my hand. I am ever mindful of the sacredness of the moment. Having listened to the supplicant's story and embraced God's love for that individual, I have a better understanding of what I am praying for and can better identify the target. My Royal Marine training is handy as I hone in on identifying any enemy lurking in the supplicant's body, mind, or spirit that must be destroyed by the precious blood of Christ and His healing gifts. I want to pray with laser accuracy for anything that is out of order to be put back in good working order by our Creator.

I confess that in some instances, I have actually googled an image of an illness that a supplicant is struggling with, to have a better understanding of the disease. I once had the privilege of praying for a woman with cancer of the upper lobe of her left lung. I was with the patient at a newer high-tech nuclear cancer unit. Her lungs and ribs were imaged and displayed on a huge TV monitor. I was able to move the cursor around the image of her rib cage and enhance the lobe with color: red for the nucleus of the cancer. I actually "saw" the cancer—the target of her healing need—and prayed into the very epicenter of it.

As a drill instructor at the rifle range of the commando training center, I oversaw some recruits who were excellent shots and earned their Marksman's Badges. Other recruits were average shots, and still others had obvious problems with hesitation or jerking or snatching the trigger. We had to work through those problems, of course. But here's the thing: if you give a marine enough ammunition, he will eventually hit the target! Using this analogy in healing prayer, we are so very fortunate because we have an endless supply of ammunition and can continue to bombard our target until we have so poured out the pure love of God that we have annihilated the enemy! This can apply to all healing prayer needs whether personal, physical, emotional, mental, financial, generational, historical, or even hysterical. In prayer, we rely upon Jesus to scope out and identify the target. As we pray into it, with our confident faith in Him, we will overcome the need with His abundant love and compassion.

I myself have been healed—have been cured. I was terminal. I was at death's door, only ten years ago, but through the prayers of thousands across the world, I was restored to life. My own resurrection from the horrors of the H1N1 swine flu virus allowed me to trade my former prayer mantra—"Lord, heal my unbelief!"—for one that better reflects my mind-set today. I know that God got me through the valley of the shadow of death. I also know from that experience that He can do all things! I now believe without doubt. My personal faith was brilliantly expanded as I crawled through the valley back to the land of the living. So today, my prayer mantra is Hebrews 11:1: "Faith is the substance of things hoped for, the evidence of things not seen" (KJV). I have become the evidence of things unseen, having had an army of faithful prayer warriors pray into reality the substance of things hoped for.

As you pray for others, please avoid using the word *just* ("Lord, *just* heal this person." "Lord, *just* help this dysfunctional family"). It is my pet peeve, but it truly is unnecessary to say it. Also please do not pray, "If it is Your will, Lord, heal this person." Think about that one. It smacks of the words of the father of the convulsive son, "if you can . . ." Jesus corrected that man! Why are you praying if you don't know that healing *is* His will? At best, it is a demonstration of weak faith; at its worst, it is evidence of a lack of knowing Jesus Christ and His healing gifts.

I am not trying to formulize how to pray, but sometimes a bit of guidance in this area can help open our eyes to see that "religious" cliché words may communicate something we do not mean. Often, after being the key speaker at an all-day or multi-day conference or mission, I'm spent. Having prayed for so very many in a short amount of time, I am exhausted and feel as though I have nothing to give. It's at these times that I truly recognize how the Lord steps in and takes over. They are the most freeing moments I have while praying for others! I am completely out of His way, and the Lord is free to do what He does best. And I get to "Amen" His work!

I'll close with the following messages of encouragement to keep us praying.

Pray continually, give thanks in all circumstances; for this is God's will for you in Christ Jesus. Do not quench the Spirit. (1 Thessalonians 5:17–19)

And the peace of God, which transcends all understanding, will guard your hearts and your minds in Christ Jesus. (Philippians 4:7)

Therefore confess your sins to each other and pray for each other so that you may be healed. The prayer of a righteous person is powerful and effective. (James 5:16)

Listen, love, and pray as the Lord directs, dear friends.

AMBASSADORS

*We are therefore Christ's ambassadors, as though
God were making his appeal through us. We implore
you on Christ's behalf: Be reconciled to God.*
—2 CORINTHIANS 5:20

In 1990, following a time of prayer with a female customer in my little picture-frame shop in Connecticut, I began praying that my hands would be as the hands of Christ. The woman who visited my place of business that day shared that she had a tremendous migraine headache. I felt led to pray for her, so I placed my hands on her head. When I had finished, much to my surprise her headache was gone! I recalled reading that Paul had prayed that he would fearlessly speak words to make the gospel known, curiously referring to himself as "an ambassador in chains" (Ephesians 6:19–20). And though I was not in chains, I related to his prayer because I desired to respond to Christ's call and passionately become an ambassador of His healing gifts, "proclaim[ing] the kingdom of God and [healing] the sick" (Luke 9:2). So it seemed good and right to pray that my hands could be used as His hands in response to that call.

As ambassadors of Christ we are called to stretch forth our hands to heal others. Yes, the Bible says that quite clearly in Acts 4:30: "Stretch out your hand to heal and perform signs and wonders through the name of your holy servant Jesus." But I love *The Message*'s translation of that passage: "Give your servants fearless confidence in preaching your Message, as you stretch out your hand to us in healings and miracles and wonders done in the name of your holy servant Jesus." Indeed, we all need fearless confidence as we preach and stretch out hands to heal in His name.

Luke 9:2 affirms the call that He has given us: "And he [Jesus] sent them out to proclaim the kingdom of God and to heal the sick." I admit that, over the years, I have challenged numerous clergypersons to not only preach the kingdom, as they are trained to do, but also to stretch forth their hands to heal the sick. As a layperson, for more than fifteen years before my ordination to the priesthood, I taught and encouraged thousands of laypeople to stretch forth their hands to heal the sick. I believe that the authority Jesus bequeathed is for all who call themselves His. How much more, then, should clergy, ordained in His name, recognize that they have Christ's authority over disease, sickness, and dis-ease?

Oftentimes when a spouse or parent requests prayer for their sick spouse or child, I anoint their hands and prescribe that they lay hands on their loved ones at least twice every day. In so doing, I am passing on Christ's healing gifts to others. I recently had the occasion to do this long distance, by telephone, with a spouse living in the UK—a man with no formal church membership, a relative unbeliever. In executing my instructions, he laid his hands several times a day upon his bride of many years, who was battling cancer. He later reported that every time he laid hands on her, her pain would subside and often disappear. He described experiencing a surprising peace in the room whenever he did this. And his wife thanked him profusely whenever he did.

I find great comfort in the fact that our Jesus placed His hands twice on a blind man at Bethsaida in order to restore his sight:

> They came to Bethsaida, and some people brought a blind man and begged Jesus to touch him. He took the blind man by the hand and led him outside the village. When he had spit on the

man's eyes and put his hands on him, Jesus asked, "Do you see anything?" He looked up and said, "I see people; they look like trees walking around." Once more Jesus put his hands on the man's eyes. Then his eyes were opened, his sight was restored, and he saw everything clearly. (Mark 8:22–25)

"Once more" Jesus put His hands on this man's eyes. Frankly, I have lost count of how many "once mores" I have had to lay hands on those whom I have prayed to be made well. This is all such a mystery. Sometimes their healing is instantaneous, and other times the "once mores" are required with perseverance. Oftentimes, in fact, for healing to be realized, it may be necessary to first unpack the causal issues (the underlying circumstances) of their dis-ease.

Many clergypersons report having vivid, and even disturbing, dreams before their ordinations.

The dream I had before my ordination was about the hands of Christ. While asleep, a day or two before my ordination to the priesthood on December 17, 2005, I saw the infant hands of Jesus, glowing and radiating light, as they gently drifted toward me. Initially the hands were outstretched as is done in the celebration of the Holy Eucharist. They were raised and extended out in what is called the Orans position. (*Orans* comes from Medieval Latin *ōrāns*, meaning one who is praying or pleading. Also, *orant* or *orante* references the posture or bodily attitude of prayer, which is usually standing, with the elbows close to the sides of the body and with the hands outstretched, tilted sideways, palms up.)

Those tiny hands steadily approached and crossed in front of me to form a *V* and landed on my heart. Beyond the *V*, I saw a chalice and a paten possessing the elements of the Lord's Supper. Then I began to see all the people for whom I had ever prayed and watched Jesus' hands compress their chests, helping them breathe, like holy CPR! As those hands came toward me slowly, again, His left hand followed

His right, and both were outstretched with palms up. The right hand was on top of His left. This deportment was akin to receiving the host in Holy Communion. Such a sacred and holy moment, I didn't want those hands to ever move away!

I believe that my dream was His loving answer to my prayers for Him to use my hands in His ministry. I had prayed that my hands might be as His hands. When I awoke I could emulate with my hands the very movements He had demonstrated. Jesus had blessed my heart, showed me how to pray for the healing of others and how I was to offer His body and blood in the Eucharist. I couldn't make this up if I tried! It was all so humbling, especially since it occurred so near to the day of my ordination.

. . .

Doctors recently discovered that I was born with a birth defect. I have one artery going into my heart, but two coming out of my heart. We are to only have one in and one out. I've always said that I'm not a theologian but a "heartalogian"; now I know why! Discovering that my heart pours out more than it takes in is an incredible image—and blessing, for one called to healing ministry. It has served to intensify my passion to share His healing gifts with all. "Bless your heart" is nearly a cliché in the South but, in my case, my heart has been blessed, indeed. Thankfully, I only discovered this recently. Had the Royal Marine Commandos known about my heart defect, I would never have been allowed to serve in Her Majesty's armed forces. God's timing is always perfect.

Dear reader, I pray that you will be empowered to "stretch out your hand to heal and perform signs and wonders through the name of your holy servant Jesus" (Acts 4:30). May Jesus' words on the cross— "Father, into your hands I commit my spirit"—be your heart's cry now (Luke 23:46). Go forth as ambassadors for Him, in Him, and through Him, allowing your healing hands to be used as His on earth.

Part Two

CHALLENGES TO HEALING

FAITH

Is anyone among you sick? Let them call the elders
of the church to pray over them and anoint them
with oil in the name of the Lord. And the prayer
offered in faith will make the sick person well.
—JAMES 5:14–15

What is the role of faith when it comes to the mystery of healing? As I have already said, I do not subscribe to "faith healing." Having enough faith to be healed is not the same as having faith without doubt in God's ability and authority to heal!

What exactly is required of supplicants when they are sick? The late Rev. Canon Jim Glennon, founder and former leader of the Healing Ministry at St. Andrew's Cathedral in Sydney, Australia, taught with conviction that all a supplicant must do is ask. "As a matter of fact, the only instruction given in the New Testament to Christians as to what they are to do when they are sick is that they are to call the elders of the church. . . . The specific thing the Christian is to do is to ask for prayer for healing."[1]

If all the sick person must do is ask for prayer regardless of confidence in God's ability to heal, then whose responsibility is it to believe, without doubt, that Jesus can and will heal? Glennon would argue that we are to look to the church and to those who profess to believe

Christ's healing gifts. According to James's prescription in chapter 5 of his letter, the sick are to call upon the elders or leaders of the church to receive prayer for healing.

Am I saying that faith is the church's responsibility? Well, yes and no. If we drill down into this matter, we will undoubtedly arrive at the conclusion that Jesus is most responsible for the measure of faith that His followers possess through His Holy Spirit (Romans 12:3). Therefore, the responsibility of the church and all who follow Christ is to obediently and unashamedly express their faith in Him, as they stretch out their hands in His name and ask Jesus to heal.

The Prayer of Faith (James 5:13–16) makes clear that God qualifies the leaders of the church to offer healing prayer to the sick. Under the kind of leadership that understands God always supplies what He commands us to do, the church can take measures to prepare to bear the burden of faith for healing in their flock. One way to get ready is for every church to offer healing prayer ministry, healing services, or healing ministry. The responsibility ultimately lies with Jesus to bestow upon His church and followers the confident faith necessary to lay hands on the sick for healing. In the name of Jesus, His church and His followers are given authority over disease and sickness.

In my experience, I have heard too many sick people say, "But I don't have enough faith to be healed." Or, "Why would God even bother with me?" Or, "Other people are far more deserving or sicker than me." Rarely have I heard these protestations rebuffed. Let's try now, shall we?

"But I don't have enough faith to be healed." Ah, if that's what is worrying you, then just follow the instructions in James 5:13–16 and ask the leaders of your church to pray for you.

"Why would God even bother with me?" Because He loves you. He made you and has never left your side since He called you by your name from your mother's womb! You are fearfully and wonderfully made (Psalm 139:14). He delights in you and longs for your love.

"Other people are far more deserving or sicker than me." No, they're not! If you alone had been the only person on earth, Jesus would still have come to assure your redemption and salvation. You are unique and precious in His sight, unlike any other person ever created.

As for the classic lament that *"I have too little faith to be healed,"* what about Lazarus? What faith did he have? None! As he was dead at the time, he couldn't even ask for prayer. And yet Jesus raised him from the dead!

Before I move on from this discussion of what God requires of the sick person to be healed, I would be remiss not to mention an important predictive characteristic of supplicants in need of healing prayer. It is called "ripeness." Ripeness, in a sick person, indicates whether they are ready to be healed or made well. As unlikely as you may find it that any supplicant would refuse—not want—to be well, I assure you that not only does this happen, it happens far more often than you might imagine.

I have stated before that Jesus did not ordain sickness. He did not cause illnesses or sicknesses to sweep across His creation and endanger the lives of the men and women He created and delights in. God is not guilty! Yet it is a fact that illnesses and diseases have flourished since Genesis, with no end in sight. Something that can increase the spread of illness is a lack of ripeness in His children.

If we do not embrace the love God has for us and choose not to love ourselves, we may reject any opportunity to be made well and restored to the fullness of life. I find that most people in this camp have a distorted image of God, seeing Him as a punishing deity that believes they deserve sickness. It may be that their family and friends have failed them in the past, but now that they're ill, they are enjoying increased attention and affection. Maybe they are so self-loathing and isolated that they cannot lift their heads even to meet Jesus' gaze. Maybe they have too closely identified with their disease and own it: my cancer, my diabetes, my heart disease, preferring what they know to what they do not know if God were to heal them. In any event, they are not ripe for healing. Until ripe, they will not ask, nor can they receive. This is a primary reason why prayer ministers wait to be asked before they pray for the supplicant. Never assume prayer is welcome.

God is all about healing, health, wholeness, and salvation. In the Greek, the word is *sozo*. In the Hebrew, it is *yeshu'a*. The question is never whether our Lord is willing to heal; the question will always come down to whether we will receive His healing.

The burden of faith in healing is in our obedience to pray in Jesus' name for healing of the sick, exercising the faith we have been given. Of course, it is glorious when supplicants also believe in Jesus and His healing gifts, but there may be undisclosed reasons why they struggle at this point. When sick people are in the active stages of disease, they may be unable to pray for themselves or receive the prayers of others. When utterly despairing from acute or chronic pain caused by their sickness or the treatment of their sickness, it is difficult, if not impossible, for the sick to fully participate in the healing process.

Why is that? If, while we pray, we are feeling a manifestation of pain, there is a tangible conflict between our pain and our confidence that God is healing us. So many patients in hospitals or nursing homes express guilt because the intensity of their pain keeps them from praying or benefiting from prayers. This is where the prayer team steps in to take on the prayer of faith for that individual. The confident faith of those called as healing prayer ministers can add their faith to the sick person's. As the burden of faith for His healing is distributed across multiple prayer ministers, the faith of the supplicant also increases.

I get such encouragement from 1 Thessalonians 5:24: "The one who calls you is faithful, and he will do it."

Read it now in *The Message*: "May God himself, the God who

makes everything holy and whole, make you holy and whole, put you together—spirit, soul, and body—and keep you fit for the coming of our Master, Jesus Christ. The One who called you is completely dependable. If he said it, he'll do it!" (1 Thessalonians 5:23–24)

The message here is bedrock for us. Paul reminds us that the New Testament is filled with assurances that it is God's will, in Christ Jesus, that we are healed: made "whole . . . put . . . together—spirit, soul, and body . . . fit for the coming of . . . Jesus Christ." The Scripture fills us with confidence that Christ is exactly who He says He is so that we can pray in faith that He will do what He has promised!

I mentioned that we would look further at the notion that Jesus is most responsible for the faith we have. That said, however, we cannot forget there is also always our part. We are commanded to stand firm, to take captive every pretension against the truth of God, to surrender all we are to all He is and make the most of every opportunity to exercise our faith in Christ and His gifts. And yet our part cannot diminish His promises. The Bible affirms that our faith, by and large, is given to us.

The apostles said to the Lord, "Increase our faith!" (Luke 17:5)

For by the grace given me I say to every one of you: Do not think of yourself more highly than you ought, but rather think of yourself with sober judgment, in accordance with the faith God has distributed to each of you. (Romans 12:3)

The Revised Standard Version reads "according to the measure of faith which God has assigned him."

For the one who was a slave when called to faith in the Lord is the Lord's freed person; similarly, the one who was free when called is Christ's slave. (1 Corinthians 7:22)

To one there is given through the Spirit a message of wisdom, to another a message of knowledge by means of the same Spirit, to another faith by the same Spirit. (1 Corinthians 12:8–9)

For it is by grace you have been saved, through faith—and this is not from yourselves, it is the gift of God. (Ephesians 2:8)

Take all the help you can get, every weapon God has issued. . . . Truth, righteousness, peace, faith, and salvation are more than words. Learn how to apply them. You'll need them throughout your life. (Ephesians 6:16–17 THE MESSAGE)

The grace of our Lord was poured out on me abundantly, along with the faith and love that are in Christ Jesus. (1 Timothy 1:14)

Though these are not all the scriptures that attest to God's gift of faith to us, these should open our eyes wide enough—and close our mouths from lamenting, if we only had enough faith . . . if this supplicant had enough faith . . . if only our church had enough faith! Consider these passages and let their words overcome our doubts and embolden us to stretch out our hands to pray for the sick with confidence, since it is "by his wounds we are healed" (Isaiah 53:5).

Let's take a look at the burden of faith for healing in four gospel stories in the Bible and one modern gospel story of healing.

- *The sick woman bore the burden of faith*—the woman with the twelve-year issue of bleeding (Matthew 9:20–22). By Jesus' own testimony, this woman's courage and faith (to push through a crowd to get to Jesus, while being identifiably "unclean" from having bled for twelve years) was the basis of her healing. It was by her faith that she was healed.
- *The four friends bore the burden of faith for the paralytic*—the

paralytic lowered though the roof by his four friends (Mark 2:1–5). We don't even know the name of this paralyzed man, much less whether he had any faith in Christ to be healed. But when Jesus was teaching in that crowded house and debris began to fall on His head, as the paralytic's four friends cut a hole in the roof and lowered their friend on a mat at Jesus' feet, there was no doubt whose faith had championed this man's healing. His friends bore the burden of faith in Christ and His healing gifts.

- *The centurion bore the burden of faith for healing*—the faith of the centurion (Matthew 8:5–13). We don't know the servant's name or how the centurion came to know of and believe Jesus' ability and willingness to heal; but we know he believed that if he simply asked Jesus to heal his servant, the servant would be made well. The centurion bore the burden of faith in Christ's ability to heal, and his servant was healed!

- *The burden of faith for healing was borne by Jesus Christ*—raising Lazarus from the dead (John 11:1–44). It was Jesus who commanded Lazarus, who had been dead for four days, to come out of the tomb. He commanded those near to remove the graveclothes so he was set free from death. When Jesus petitioned His Father in prayer, Lazarus was raised from the dead.

- *The body of Christ (the church-at-large) bore the burden of faith for healing.* In October 2009, a priest lay comatose and near to death when word spread across the world, rallying those who believe Jesus and His healing gifts to pray for a miracle for Nigel Mumford. After emerging from a coma in December 2009, I felt as I suspect Lazarus must have. Unaware of the time that had passed, weakened, and confused—I discovered that thousands upon thousands of God's faith-filled children had prayed for me to be restored. The burden of faith for my healing was upon the body of Christ, the church-at-large. Being comatose, I could not pray.

What is the role of the supplicant, sick person, or patient?

- Do I have the faith of the woman with the issue of blood for my own healing?
- Do I have friends or a prayer team with the faith for me to be healed?
- Do I have the centurion's faith to believe for a friend or family member's healing?
- Do I believe that Jesus Christ Himself will supply all of my needs?
- Do I believe the body of Christ can rally to advocate for my healing?

Who bears the burden of faith for healing?

- My own profound faith that enables me to seek Jesus in prayer for even myself
- A group of friends who will storm the Throne Room for my healing
- One friend of deep faith who intercedes for me before Jesus
- Jesus Christ Himself
- The body of Christ / church-at-large

In closing, the burden of bearing faith for healing is summed up in Galatians 6:2. I especially appreciate the Amplified Version of this verse: "Carry one another's burdens and in this way you will fulfill the requirements of the law of Christ [that is, the law of Christian love]."

The genesis of faith in Jesus Christ and His healing gifts is a gift of God, while the burden of faith for healing to be realized in this life is borne by all who call themselves His and obey His call to lay hands on the sick so they are made well.

DESIRE

When Jesus saw him stretched out by the
pool and knew how long he had been there,
he said, "Do you want to get well?"
—JOHN 5:6 THE MESSAGE

Long lines for prayer at our healing services and our appointment calendars regularly filled with the names of folks seeking healing prayer do not always portend a genuine desire to be healed. Who knows? It can be difficult to ascertain supplicants' resistance to healing because often they themselves don't even know if they want it!

When I take prayer appointments, I try to discern the answer to this question: "Do you want to be healed?" I've even been known to take off my wristwatch and hold it out to supplicants before laying hands on them, asking them straightaway: "If this watch represents your healing, what do you have to do?" Most supplicants intent upon healing will immediately grab hold of my watch.

Healing ministers should be aware that not all who present themselves for prayer truly desire to be healed. What a conundrum! When we consider the many blocks to receiving healing, we must never forget the possibility that a commonplace, self-induced block is lurking about—a supplicant's personal resistance to healing.

Jesus Christ is the same today as He was yesterday and will be tomorrow. Christ, literally, grabbed the attention of that invalid at the pool who had been forced to "sit out" his healing opportunities due to his lameness, while others got into the pool before him. Jesus also had the attention of the woman with an issue of blood for twelve long years as she crouched amid a crowd waiting to reach for the hem of His garment and be healed as He passed by. Today Jesus continues to grab the attention of those who passionately desire to be healed. Jesus Christ got attention wherever He went, and He still does. We simply need to be alert and expectant to receive healing.

. . .

The moment I saw it, I was drawn like a magnet to a 1566 painting by the Italian Renaissance master Paolo Veronese entitled *Barnabas Curing the Sick*. St. Barnabas is depicted holding an open Bible over the head of a sick man. It reminded me of chapter 8 in Matthew's gospel, when a Roman centurion humbly asked Jesus to pray for his beloved ill servant. Jesus offered to come to the soldier's house where the servant was, but in an act of incredible faith, "The centurion replied, 'Lord, I do not deserve to have you come under my roof. But just say the word, and my servant will be healed'" (v. 8). "Then Jesus said to the centurion, 'Go! Let it be done just as you believed it would.' And his servant was healed at that moment" (v. 13).

Just say the word! In Veronese's painting the Word is hovering over the head of a visibly ill man. I have held the Bible over people in a similar fashion as I prayed. I envision the Word being poured into the minds of those supplicants. With His Word overcoming their minds, I imagine our Lord saying, "Let it be done as you believed it would." I believe with every fiber of my being that as the supplicant believes Jesus and is willing to receive, Jesus is healing!

At the beginning of this chapter, I quoted John 5:6. Jesus spotted a man who had been lame, an invalid for thirty-eight years. A few commentaries speculate that the man had sinned and had been cast out of his community in shame. A common block to receiving healing is when one lives with shame and the feeling of being unworthy. Thus, if correct in their assessment, this man likely had never been forgiven or had never forgiven himself. In healing ministry, supplicants bound by unforgiveness have a giant block to healing. Not forgiving oneself can cause a person to resist healing. Those who struggle with unforgiveness feel unworthy and, therefore, will resist genuinely desiring their healing.

Jesus interacted with the lame man at the side of the pool by saying those truly amazing words: "Do you want to be made well?"

When I meet people like the lame man at the pool, I often ask them the same question, "Do you want to be healed?" I've had some interesting responses! Some answer with wide, staring eyes trained on me as if I had just exposed a nerve or put a knife to their open wound. Sadly, some people have so closely taken on the identity of sickness that they have no concept of who they used to be, who they are at present, or who they might become. Some are so enmeshed in the identity of the disease that they fear that, if healed, they would lose the obliged pitiable attention of others. Some wrestle with the possibility that if they were to be healed they might also lose their financial benefits and compensation in addition to the love and compassion of those who care for them.

Sadly, still others relish their affliction, wallowing in misery, content with their pain in exchange for the benefit of favored attention. When I meet with folks such as these, I truly have to pluck up the courage to ask them, "Do you want to be healed?" It makes me so uncomfortable to ask this. But if I discern that their condition may be something they cherish more than the prospect of healing, I obey the Lord and ask the hard question. Given my counsel to healing ministers and my personal penchant to "listen, love, and pray," asking this question seems out of bounds. I do ask, however, with extreme caution and only out of God's love for the supplicant who appears to have been seduced by sickness. The question then arises, can we pray for and help those who do not want that help?

I met with a woman who spoke for twenty minutes about her life of rejection. She listed everyone she could think of who had rejected her—father, mother, sisters, brother, teachers, aunts, uncles, and so on. The list seemed endless. As I listened I was shocked to "see," in the Spirit, my name at the bottom of her long list! I'd been puzzled by her hostility and aggression toward me from the get-go, particularly since we'd never met before. The Spirit showed me, however, that her behavior was a ploy to take the upper hand in our prayer time—to reject me before I could reject her. Her modus operandi and defense mechanism were to keep people at arm's length so as not to be rejected. Perhaps she had even made an inner vow to reject others before they could reject her. This was how she lived every day of her life!

With the Spirit's prompting, I described to her the picture I had seen of her list of "rejecters," with my name at the bottom. I told her that I was not going to allow her to reject me. I used the very words of Jesus, who assured us, "I will never leave you or reject you." I told her that under no circumstance would I allow her to include me on that list. The look on her face was priceless. A mix of "Uh-oh, I've been found out" and "Wow, someone is actually listening to me!" It was a sacred moment for us both. I stuck by my word, and she eventually rejected her default coping mechanism of rejecting others. She learned to receive the love of Christ and others. She allowed herself to be loved. Her identity was changed. She had been wallowing in self-pity for years, much like the man at the pool.

The lame man responded to Jesus: "Sir, I have no one to put me in the water; people push in front of me." The whole premise of "healing" that this man and all the others desired at the pool was based on superstition. They believed an angel visited the pool and stirred up the waters so that the first person in would be healed! Of course, it was a natural wonder, perhaps similar to Wekiva and Rock Springs, in Apopka, Florida, where deep, lengthy fissures in the pools' limestone bottoms discharge forty-five million gallons of water to "boil" and bubble up each day. Even today, the sick make pilgrimages to waters widely believed to possess healing qualities. Ever heard of Warm Springs, Georgia, frequented by President Franklin D. Roosevelt to alleviate paralytic pain? What about the mineral springs at Saratoga Springs, New York, founded in 1776? And let's not overlook the granddaddy of miracles: the Grottos at Lourdes, France, where sick people drink or bathe in the waters flowing from their springs.

Jesus asked the question, "Do you want to be healed?" He sure didn't seem uncomfortable when He asked. Even commentaries that believe the man was a whiner and projected blame on others, recognize that this lame man had unconfessed sin. If the man had unconfessed sin, then he certainly struggled with unforgiveness. Those who are not able to forgive others are notoriously unable to forgive themselves. Hence, Jesus readily understood that this lame man had a major block to healing. That's why our Lord could ask him that difficult question. It wasn't to convict the man as much as it was to open him to receive Christ's love and healing.

The "rejected" woman, like the lame man at the pool, had some hefty forgiving to do—even forgiving herself! Friends, I submit to you that unforgiveness can cripple the strongest of men and women. Unforgiveness is an emotional cancer that rots out the very core of our existence.

Perhaps one or more of your supplicants carry around inside the knowledge and memory of an offense that is rotting their life. Perhaps they continue to give great power to their perpetrator(s). Or perhaps they are living with a victim's mentality—"Stuck by the pool," unable to access healing. Or are they living defensively, like the "rejected" woman, allowing self-defense mechanisms to sap their life's energy? They need to know that only through Jesus Christ can they be set free.

Jesus came to set captives free. Through prayer and conversation, the "rejected" woman moved from victim to victor to victory.

Jesus stepped in on the Sabbath, a day where even healing was viewed as work. What an amazing surprise for that lame man, suddenly able to walk, to pick up his meager belongings and be able to function.

We now know the outcome of the rejected woman I prayed with. She became a new woman healed of all rejection. She now lives in her right mind.

We know the outcome of the man by the pool. He was set free. Cured, able to walk upright for all to see!

And we know the outcome of Jesus' crucifixion: His resurrection and our healing won!

Here is a challenge for supplicants struggling with the desire to be healed:

So you've prayed to God that He will take your pain away, but it just seems as if He wants you to carry that cross forever. Have you ever thought that perhaps God really does want to heal you, but you're actually standing in the way? Tom Mann's book *Do You Want to Be Healed? Allowing God to Heal Brokenness in Your Life* shares a little-known truth about Jesus' healing ministry: you have to be ready for healing before Jesus will heal you. That means you can't keep one foot in your dysfunction while crying out to God for help. You have to go all in before Jesus can perform that healing miracle in your life. If you're ready for that kind of commitment—ready for Jesus to wipe away your tears and heal the brokenness in your soul—take a chance and say, yes, I want to be healed.[1]

Are you ready to go "all in"?

Are you ready for that kind of commitment, ready for Jesus to wipe away every tear?

Are you sick and tired of being sick and tired?

What's holding you back?
Do you not see that the sickness that afflicts you is your enemy?
Or have you made it your BFF?
Do you desire to be healed and set free?
Do you want to be made well?

Then, dear friend:

Choose life.
Choose the Author of life.
Choose the Way, the Truth, and the Life.
Choose His forgiveness.
Choose His love.
Choose His healing.
Choose Jesus Christ!

10

ROADBLOCKS

Be very careful, then, how you live—not as unwise
but as wise, making the most of every opportunity,
because the days are evil. Therefore do not be
foolish, but understand what the Lord's will is.
—Ephesians 5:15–17

There are many roadblocks to receiving Christ's gift of healing by faith, either as a healing minister or the one seeking healing. In this chapter we will look first at three primary emotional responses that inhibit healing—doubt, anxiety, and fear.

Emotions That Inhibit Healing

When we doubt the Lord's existence or His love, will, trustworthiness, faithfulness, or power, we become riddled with anxiety. As Paul pointed out, our thinking becomes futile when we are overcome by a lack of confidence in God's divine nature (Romans 1). Perhaps, by its fruit, we can best understand the futility of anxiety. Contrast the fruit of God's Spirit (love, joy, peace, patience, kindness, goodness, faithfulness, gentleness, and self-control from Galatians 5:22–23) with the rotted fruit of anxiety and fear. When doubt persists, it sows anxiety and reaps fear!

Doubt

What does Jesus say about doubt?

[Jesus said]"Truly I tell you, if anyone says to this mountain, 'Go, throw yourself into the sea,' and does not doubt in their heart but believes that what they say will happen, it will be done for them." (Mark 11:23)

He [Jesus] said to them [His disciples], "Why are you troubled, and why do doubts rise in your minds?" (Luke 24:38)

[During Peter's attempt to walk on water to reach Jesus.] "Immediately Jesus reached out his hand and caught him. 'You of little faith,' he [Jesus] said, 'why did you doubt?'" (Matthew 14:31)

Then he [Jesus] said to Thomas, "Put your finger here; see my hands. Reach out your hand and put it into my side. Stop doubting and believe." (John 20:27)

Now let's look at what James said about the downside of doubt:

If any of you lacks wisdom, you should ask God, who gives generously to all without finding fault, and it will be given to you. But when you ask, you must believe and not doubt, because the one who doubts is like a wave of the sea, blown and tossed by the wind. That person should not expect to receive anything from the Lord. Such a person is double-minded and unstable in all they do. (James 1:5–8)

Before any of us despairs over James's harsh assessment of doubters, I would remind us that we've all been there. We all have doubted Christ at some time in our lives but can now rejoice in His healing of our doubt.

In his only letter included in the Bible, Jude prompts us to deal gently with those who doubt: "Be merciful to those who doubt" (Jude v. 22). Jude's words are akin to a cool breeze tempering the heat of humiliation caused by our doubting. Both writers are correct, but only when they are weighed together and balanced on Jesus' scales. Enter Jesus and the father of the boy with an impure spirit:

> Jesus asked the boy's father, "How long has he been like this?"
>
> "From childhood," he answered. "It has often thrown him into fire or water to kill him. But *if you can* do anything, take pity on us and help us."
>
> "*If* you can?" said Jesus. "Everything is possible for one who believes."
>
> Immediately the boy's father exclaimed, "I do believe; help me overcome my unbelief!" (Mark 9:21–24, emphasis added)

This passage warms my heart every time I read it. In the end, after the spirit left the boy, he appeared dead—like a corpse—until Jesus reached down, took his hand, and lifted him up, at which point the boy stood up.

Doubt is always the result of unbelief. We need to be healed of our unbelief even when we believe. Sometimes our faith in Christ is credible for His ability to do certain things but is weak regarding His ability to do other things. Jesus wants you to believe Him, period. Our faith is to be void of doubt.

When we do not believe Him, we doubt Him. And when we doubt Him, we become anxious.

Anxiety

Paul's final exhortation in his letter to the Philippians addresses our common temptation to be anxious as well as our need for healing from it. Imagine that Paul wrote these words while he was being held captive, within the walls of a prison:

> Rejoice in the Lord always. I will say it again: Rejoice! Let your gentleness be evident to all. The Lord is near. Do not be anxious about anything, but in every situation, by prayer and petition, with thanksgiving, present your requests to God. And the peace of God, which transcends all understanding, will guard your hearts and your minds in Christ Jesus. (Philippians 4:4–7)

Let's unpack this powerful paragraph.

"Rejoice in the Lord always. I will say it again: Rejoice!"
Paul commands us to rejoice, not once, but twice! How can we rejoice in every situation of life? Is that even possible? Well, no . . . not exactly; but yes, in Christ! God intends that we see our circumstances through His eyes. A horse will follow the direction of his rider's eyes. If the horse and rider are traversing a narrow trail overhanging a cliff and the rider looks over the side, the horse will get perilously close to the edge. So the rider must keep his eyes trained on where he wants to go, on the safe path ahead. Similarly, Paul's command that we rejoice requires us to keep our eyes focused on our trustworthy Lord so we're not overcome by what is happening around us. Rejoicing (from the transliterated Greek verb *chairo*), arises from our joy whenever we focus on God's grace and love during our circumstances, praising Him for His faithful presence in our lives.

Philippians 4:4–7 is an excellent passage to memorize if you suffer from anxiety. Remember that Paul is not making a request, he is commanding us: "You rejoice. Keep your eyes on the truth, who is Christ Jesus, and you will have no other response than to rejoice in Him!"

"Let your gentleness be evident to all."

Are you a bull in a china shop? Do you come across as aggressive and combative? Hmm . . . the antidote to aggressive behavior is given to everyone who manifests the fruit of the Spirit. Yes, gentleness is a fruit harvested from the gift of the Holy Spirit (Galatians 5:23), who is given to us through faith in Christ. I promise we'll explore the Holy Spirit's role later on.

First Timothy 6:11 says, "But you, man of God, flee from all this, and *pursue* righteousness, godliness, faith, love, endurance, and *gentleness*" (emphasis added). Perhaps it is time to pursue the fruit of gentleness. I would suggest that if aggression and belligerence are outwardly present, very likely there is considerable guilt and self-condemnation going on internally. The Lord would say to us: *Be at peace, dear souls. Allow faith in Me to grow and heal your doubt, anxiety, and fear.*

"The Lord is near."

If we do not believe that God is a person, but rather just a dumb deity that is distant and unconcerned with us, then we are predisposed to regularly manifest doubt, anxiety, and fear reactions. On the contrary, our God is a loving, caring person, who is ever present and passionately concerned about us!

> [God said] "No one will be able to stand against you all the days of your life. As I was with Moses, so I will be with you; I will never leave you nor forsake you." (Joshua 1:5)

> [God said] "Can a mother forget the baby at her breast and have no compassion on the child she has borne? Though she may forget, I will not forget you!" (Isaiah 49:15)

> [Jesus said] "And surely I am with you always, to the very end of the age." (Matthew 28:20)

Think about that last verse for a moment: *Jesus is always with you.* Whatever you are doing, He is there. Even as you read this book, He is with you. The late Leanne Payne, author and healing minister, taught how to practice His Presence by closing your eyes, placing one hand over your heart, being aware of its gentle beating, and feeling the rise and fall of your chest as you draw breath. Won't you try this now, in faith knowing that He is truly with you?

"Do not be anxious about anything."

Okay, Paul—can you hear us yelling "Uncle"? Phew! Yep, God, we do hear You, we do hear Your command! We hear Your voice, loud and clear, through the words of a man chained to a prison wall, writing to implore us not to be anxious about anything. Even Peter, in his first letter contained in the Bible, concurred with Paul: "Cast all your anxiety on him [Christ] because he cares for you" (1 Peter 5:7).

By faith, and in total trust, we want to obey God. So, let's believe He is able to calm the storm in our hearts and minds. He does hear and answer us when we call upon Him. Let's thank Him for giving us His peace to replace our anxious thoughts, even at this very moment. Amen?

"But in every situation, by prayer and petition, with
thanksgiving, present your requests to God."

Paul is giving us the prescription to defeat anxiety: pray with thanksgiving! Ask; give thanks; and leave it all to God: "Please take it, it's too heavy for me; but not for You. Giving it all to You, laying it at Your feet. Oh, thank You, thank You, dear Lord!" Don't forget the thanksgiving bit either! We've learned that the only way to be at peace is to obey His instructions and give thanks. Paul reminds us to "pray continually, give thanks in all circumstances; for this is God's will for you in Christ Jesus. Do not quench the Spirit" (1 Thessalonians 5:17–19).

"And the peace of God, which transcends
all understanding, will guard your hearts
and your minds in Christ Jesus."

Ah, we've come to the prized fruit—peace! It is said that we must go out on a limb to get to the fruit. But, honestly, how much risk is it to go out onto a limb that God has provided and will support by His strength? There is always, and only, an upside to resting on His promises.

Anxiety is a response triggered by haunted thoughts and emotions from our pasts. Don't allow the past to ruin your present or your future. Override those involuntary responses, once dependent upon your collusion, by instead choosing His peace. Will you suffer setbacks along the way? Of course, but every time you choose peace you bolster your new default reaction to exercise free will and choose to trust Christ to bestow upon you His peace.

> [Jesus said] "Peace I leave with you; my peace I give you. I do not give to you as the world gives. Do not let your hearts be troubled and do not be afraid." (John 14:27)

Fear

Oh no! How have we arrived at the f-bomb—that vulgar four-letter word: f-e-a-r? We shouldn't be here, should we? If we'd obeyed God's instructions and put down doubt and rejected anxiety, we'd be lying on a beach somewhere, listening to gentle waves lapping the shore, feeling the warmth of the sun on our peaceful, totally relaxed bodies. Instead, here we are—and all because when doubt persists, it sows anxiety and reaps fear.

Our sense of fear goes all the way back to the garden of Eden when, after disobeying God by eating the forbidden fruit, the first man and woman's nakedness suddenly mutated to nudity; causing them to hide in great fear when they heard God calling them to fellowship with Him in the cool of the evening. Fear has launched a thousand ships, so to speak—fear of sailing off the edge of the earth; fear of falling from a great height; fear of dreaded news; fear of failure; fear of success; fear of the unknown; fear of death; fear of saying "I love you"; fear of the dark; fear of forgiving; fear of accepting Christ and losing control. The list is endless.

But in every instance where fear reigns, we will always find that its forerunners of doubt and anxiety have been its instigators.

Fear can be debilitating, robbing us of His peace. I have always had butterflies. Okay, I'll call it what it is. I've always felt fear before preaching, teaching, or speaking. I was very introverted as a child, and that child still intimidates me when I must "perform." Thankfully, I'm fine as soon as I open my mouth, but I have come to see those butterflies as God's reminder that His Spirit needs to regain control of my whole being, especially as He sharpens me in readiness to proclaim His Word.

I find it helpful to replace perceived fear in my life with relevant scriptures that can cut off fearful thoughts before they overcome my person. For instance:

[Jesus said] "But seek first his kingdom and his righteousness, and all these things will be given to you as well. Therefore do not worry about tomorrow, for tomorrow will worry about itself. Each day has enough trouble of its own." (Matthew 6:33–34)

[Jesus said] "Don't be afraid; just believe." (Mark 5:36)

For I [Paul] have learned to be content whatever the circumstances. I know what it is to be in need, and I know what it is to have plenty. I have learned the secret of being content in any and every situation. . . . I can do all this through him who gives me strength. (Philippians 4:11–13)

Strengthen the feeble hands, steady the knees that give way; say to those with fearful hearts, "Be strong, do not fear; your God will come." (Isaiah 35:3–4)

Another way to invoke a default or go-to place is to physically move our eyes heavenward and seek God when we first begin to feel fear. Recall how a horse is safely led by the direction of his rider's eyes remaining focused on the safe path ahead. So it is with us also. The safe path is always His path, so endeavor to remain focused on Him. Seek first His kingdom.

When we are in dire straits and cry out to the Lord, He does hear us. His answer, though unique to each of us, will always culminate in peace. We can be certain that God will either change our circumstances *or* change us to empower us to stand firm. I am rejoicing as I write, that our Jesus was empowered to finish His mission and secure our forgiveness, salvation, and peace.

Becoming an Overcomer

Let's summarize a process by which we can allow God to help our supplicants get around the emotional roadblocks of doubt, anxiety, and fear and be set free. Counsel them to:

Step 1. Invite Jesus Christ into your wound(s) and ask Him to set you free from them.

Step 2. Seek medical help. Ask Jesus to guide, direct, and bless your path of healing.

Step 3. Get engaged in reading God's Word. You will not believe or love whom you do not know. Seek to intimately know Jesus and His nature.

Step 4. Create a 9-1-1 list of strategies that help deliver you from doubt, anxiety, and fear, and can bring you to the safety of His peace. Make this list when you are not afraid. Add scriptures to it and the names and contact info of friends who will encourage them.

Step 5. Practice the principle of substitution. The moment you become aware that you are in the presence of doubt, anxiety, or fear, stop yourself! Stop dead in your tracks and physically look up, seeking first the kingdom of God by saying: "Thank You, God, for this reminder of You." In so doing you will be securing a paradigm shift in your body and in your mind: establishing God's authority over your thinking and attendant emotions.

Many of our supplicants are enslaved by the familiar spirits of doubt, anxiety, and fear. It truly is a form of enslavement, isn't it? After all, we've all been coached to "listen to our gut." But should we listen to those high-alert emotional responses to doubt, anxiety, and fear that falsely alert our guts that we are "under attack"? Couldn't such intense responses be the result of learned behaviors that can be unlearned?

It is commonly held that it only takes twenty-one days to break a habit. I put it to you that if your supplicants will follow what I am about to suggest, they will get their joy back, and their doubt, anxiety, and fear responses will become a thing of the past. As a minister of healing, having worked with hundreds of people who have shared, over the years, that they were set free, I wholeheartedly commend this biblically based process to you!

There is a simple premise involved in this process of healing; that is, we can redirect to the Lord every doubtful, anxious, and fearful thought and replace each one with His thoughts. We can substitute a negative thought with a positive thought, again and again, until at the expense of our old, toxic thought patterns we have retrained our minds to default to God's Spirit within us.

In effect, for twenty-one days we will take every thought captive and cause it to yield to Jesus Christ. Let's consult Paul, once again, to get his take on this paradigm: "We demolish arguments and every pretension that sets itself up against the knowledge of God, and we take captive every thought to make it obedient to Christ" (2 Corinthians 10:5).

Faithfully working through this for twenty-one consecutive days will create a new habit of giving God the glory and not paying homage to those old tape recordings of "stinkin thinkin" from years ago.

Putting on this new habit will change the landscape of our lives. No longer will we sit under a dark cloud of uncertainty, expecting the proverbial "other shoe" to drop on us. Instead we will gradually see that cloud dissipate, and the Light of the World, which is another name for Jesus, will break through! Day by day, substitute every negative thought with a positive, truth-filled thought—even when the only positive thought to rebut your negative thoughts is, *"I am fearfully and wonderfully made"* . . . I know that full well from Psalm 139:14!

The truth is that God never wanted us to live under this cloud, nor did He ever want us to live with oppression. Jesus came to set the captives free and to give us life in abundance. We can be set free now. We can take captive every errant thought, look up, and say, "Thank You, God, for this reminder of You," then replace every negative thought with one that honors Him and His unfailing love.

Nevertheless, your supplicants may still find themselves heading down the doubt, anxiety, and fear road occasionally. Remind them not to worry. Life happens. But as soon as they realize they are going in the wrong direction again, they should stop themselves. In any case, they need to know to not beat up on themselves. As soon as possible, have them shake the dust off their sandals from their detour and get back on the road God has laid out for their recovery and healing.

Behaviors and Beliefs That Undermine Our Faith

In addition to the emotional roadblocks to healing of doubt, anxiety, and fear, there are many more I classify as having more to do with how we act, what we believe, and the circumstance in which we find ourselves. What they all have in common, however, is that they are able to derail or stop healing in its tracks. Here are a few I believe are most apt to be present in supplicants seeking healing.

Unforgiveness

I would argue that unforgiveness is the most common of all blocks to healing. I've already devoted a chapter to this topic, but what follows is an abridged look at this particular impediment. Christ's own words help us understand the importance of overcoming this block. Contained in the Lord's Prayer are these words: "Forgive us our trespasses as we forgive those who trespass against us." The Lord's Prayer, recited in many church services, is adapted from Jesus' prayer as found in Luke 11:4: "Forgive us our sins, for we also forgive everyone who sins against us." Jesus said: "Forgive, and you will be forgiven" (Luke 6:37). He elaborated on this: "And when you stand praying, if you hold anything against anyone, forgive them, so that your Father in heaven may forgive you your sins" (Mark 11:25).

God has forgiven us. If we don't forgive, we are putting ourselves above God. Ask your supplicants to reflect on this a moment to discern whether unforgiveness has found a safe haven in their spirits and souls. It may be lurking behind what deceptively appears to be justifiable. But in Christ's love, hear this: our inability to forgive is never justifiable. He commanded us to forgive, lest we ourselves cannot be forgiven. We don't wait to feel like forgiving, nor can we wait for our offenders to be worthy of forgiveness. This is non-negotiable! We should get rid of any trace of this—clean it up as soon as possible.

A common fallacy about forgiveness is that we must first feel generous or charitable toward an offender or understand why an offender did what they did, or be ready to be reconciled to the perpetrator. To forgive as Christ commands is never dependent upon our feelings or our understanding. Jesus used one translated Greek word, *aphiemi*, whenever He commanded us to forgive. The bottom line is that if we do not forgive, then we are not forgiven.

Suggest to your supplicants that they ask Jesus to be present and reflect on whether there is any experience, event, or episode that wounded, offended, or scarred their life. If something pops into their mind, have them ponder who is attached to that wound, offense, or scar. After identifying them, they should ask themselves whether they've ever properly forgiven them and asked Jesus to also forgive them. If they have not, they should do so now. Even if they've previously done this, since it resurfaced during this exercise, that wound, offense, or scar may not be fully healed.

Inner Vows and Bitter Roots

An inner vow arises out of pledges we make with ourselves: to do, feel, or think something or not to do, feel, or think something. An inner vow can become a bitter root or vice versa. Roots of bitterness often occur when we judge others or ourselves harshly without mercy. Both inner vows and bitter roots can be so subtle and understated that we may not even remember them.

When inner vows and roots of bitterness are triggered, however, they can be masked as a proverb, axiom, or adage that sounds falsely reasonable and judicious. Though our conscious minds may not recall their genesis, our actions, emotions, or thoughts may be under their control.

"I will never do that again." "I will never trust again." "I will never love again." These are examples of inner vows that appear to be harmless on their surface. Unfortunately, they are enormously powerful and can defeat our lives and liberty in Christ. During a teaching on inner vows and bitter roots, a fellow healing minister just couldn't grasp this topic. On her long drive home after class, she cried out to the Lord to help her understand, and He disclosed four distinct vignettes from her life. Amazingly, in explaining this topic to her, the Lord also healed her mightily.

Scene 1 (age five): *Her father towered over her as she sat motionless in a big fireside chair.* As he lectured her, she perceived that he believed she lacked good sense and judgment. Feeling browbeaten, she deflected this "assault" by consciously rolling her eyes and sighing deeply.

Scene 2 (age eight): *Her father's birthday dinner.* He was pleased to open her small gift that she had bought "with her own money." Then he opened a big gift from her mother, a housewife. Her father was elated by her mother's gift of a golf bag. She felt warmth rise from her neck to her cheeks as this thought formed in her mind: *Huh! I spent my own money. Mom doesn't even work! She "bought" his gift with his money! That's not fair!*

Scene 3 (age twenty): *She phoned home to say that she decided to stay for dinner at her girlfriend's home.* Her father exploded into the phone, "You decided? Get home!"

Scene 4 (age fifty): *A housewife, mother of three children, carrying folded laundry as she passes by her husband at his desk reconciling their bank accounts.* He asked, "Hey honey, why is there a fifty-dollar check to XYZ?" She rolled her eyes, sighed heavily, and sarcastically retorted, "Oh my, did that fifty-dollar check break the bank?" Her shocked husband asked, "What did I say to offend you?" Walking away, over her shoulder she countered, "It's not what you said; it's how you said it!"

These four scenes spanning her life lucidly attest the ingathered pain of her forgotten inner vows and latent bitter roots. Let's dig deeper in this recap:

Scenes 1 and 3: My friend capitulated to her father's appraisal that she lacked good sense and judgment. Despite multiple concrete proofs that her perception of her father's opinion was unfounded, she clung to this lie for five decades! Her inner vow and, ultimately, the bitter root was "I lack good judgment skills and I'm incapable of making wise decisions."

Scene 2: A root of bitterness against her mother nurtured an inner vow to "never spend money I didn't earn myself!" The Lord showed my friend that both this bitter root and inner vow had morphed into her lifelong inability to graciously accept gifts and compliments from anyone.

Scene 4: In God's mercy, this scene magnifies the painful impact of inner vows and bitter roots on her whole life. A harmless inquiry by her husband triggered her to feel guilt and shame for having spent money she had not earned! She had done what she had vowed never to do.

In making vows, we attempt to close ourselves off from revisiting certain actions, feelings, or thoughts. We vow to "never" or sometimes "always" _____ (fill in the blank). With misguided self-preservation, we pledge to never be put in that situation again. We erect high walls to keep us safe and fail to see the prison in which we have confined ourselves.

Hebrews 12:15 says, "See to it . . . that no bitter root grows up to cause trouble and defile many." The English word *defile* used here is translated from the Greek verb *miainó* (Strong's #3392) and is defined as "to stain—as in to pollute the soul, defile, corrupt, figuratively rendering something morally or spiritually defiled."

In light of the warning, suggest to your supplicants that they ask the Lord to reveal any inner vows and bitter roots that may be hiding from His truth. If He shows them, they should ask Him to remove them so that they can freely receive His healing.

Unworthiness

Sadly, I meet many people who do not believe they are worthy to be healed. Even when they confess that God loves them and that Christ died for them to be healed, they are entrenched in narratives such as: "There are so many people out there who are far worse off than me." "I've lived such a sinful life, why should God heal me?" "Who am I that God would heal me?" "I don't deserve to be healed."

Indeed, they can even parse Scripture to support their narrative, for example, "So you also, when you have done everything you were told to do, should say, 'We are unworthy servants; we have only done our duty'" (Luke 17:10), and "That is why I did not even consider myself worthy to come to you. But just say the word, and my servant will be healed" (Luke 7:7).

These passages cite our unworthiness, but their intent is to point us to God, who loves us and sent Jesus to die for us, so that out of His worthiness we could be made worthy. Of course, we are not worthy! There is not one who is worthy by his or her own measure. But those who believe in Jesus Christ and have accepted His sacrifice for them—they have been made worthy!

Look again at the last words quoted in Luke 7:7: "But just say the word, and my servant will be healed." Just say the word and we will be healed! Neither God's love nor His healing is the result of our worthiness. What exactly motivated Jesus to heal the centurion's servant? Was it his worthiness? Of course not! It was the centurion's faith that Jesus could heal.

Read now Matthew 15:25–28:

The woman came and knelt before him. "Lord, help me!" she said. He replied, "It is not right to take the children's bread and toss it to the dogs." "Yes it is, Lord," she said. "Even the dogs eat the crumbs that fall from their master's table." Then Jesus said to her,

"Woman, you have great faith! Your request is granted." And her daughter was healed at that moment.

Again, we see that healing is not the result of our worthiness, but it is born out of our faith in Jesus that He can—and will—heal!

It breaks my heart when people in need of healing are riddled with feelings of total unworthiness and demur from seeking His intervention. They feel forgotten and cast aside as their negative mind-set takes over. It is as though they have written themselves out of God's Book of Life. This is so terribly wrong and utterly sad. It is not the promise of Jesus.

A Scripture passage comes to mind that offers a remedy. Here are Jesus' words in John 10:9–10: "I am the gate; whoever enters through me will be saved. They will come in and go out, and find pasture. The thief comes only to steal and kill and destroy; I have come that they may have life, and have it to the full."

This clearly tells us that Jesus came that we may have life to the full—abundantly! Jesus even identifies that anything—any thought, word, or deed that steals, kills, and destroys—is a thief and is most certainly not from Him. Think about it: we can choose to wallow in a lie that our God doesn't care and has rejected us or choose to live in His abundance.

If your supplicants say they love Jesus, the question then is, have they made their home in Him? Then they should embrace this verse from Romans that ministers to me every day. It encourages me to keep on keeping on, because it declares that what I may struggle with has been defeated by the one who knows me best and loves me most. We all, ministers and supplicants alike, should hang on to these wonderful words: "Therefore, there is now no condemnation for those who are in Christ Jesus, because through Christ Jesus the law of the Spirit who gives life has set you free from the law of sin and death" (Romans 8:1–2).

Beloved, we are not condemned; we are loved beyond measure! Jesus died so that we may have life in abundance. Jesus is not who condemns us and makes us feel unworthy. Such thoughts are erroneous beliefs about Christ that block His truth and, consequently, block our healing. Implore your supplicants not to wallow in them but to confess their thoughts, and ask Jesus to remove them and fill them with the spirit of truth. When we are communing with the God Almighty, we know that we are loved, forgiven, and made worthy by His wounds to receive all His precious promises—including healing!

Some years ago, I was asked to speak at Gordon Conwell College in Boston. I honestly wasn't looking forward to it, as I'd heard that the nearly one thousand students who would attend could chew up a speaker. I called my mentor, Francis MacNutt, and pled, "Help!" He laughed at me. I reminded him that he was supposed to be my spiritual director and I needed his counsel. He laughed even more. Hearing my increased anxiety, he finally said, "Nigel, calm down. Look at my wife, Judith; whenever she speaks she smiles, she makes eye contact with the audience, she just enjoys telling people about Jesus. I have two words for you, Nigel: 'Have fun!'"

"But I'm British," I protested. Then we both laughed. Since that time, I truly have had fun. I needed to be given permission to enjoy my life and the work God has given me to do. Thank you, Francis!

Now I'm asking you to give those you minister to permission to have fun! Insist they stop carrying a cross God never gave them. Remind them that if you are in Christ, you have been made worthy by His sacrifice. Pray that they will receive His love and will return it. Oh, may the sheer joy of our Lord Jesus Christ be your strength and their strength!

A Negative Approach

Do some of your supplicants tend to think in a negative way? Do they usually see a glass as half empty? Do they dwell on adversity and disenchantment? In my experience, I have encountered negativity as a major block to healing. There is a reason that the gospel of Jesus Christ is called good news: Nowhere in Jesus Christ do we find naysaying, whining, grumbling, and defeatism. Christ is our victor. Not even death could hold Him down.

I shall never forget meeting with a woman for twenty minutes before asking her to go home. In that short time she had totally worn me out. From our first introductions I felt her suck all the oxygen out of the room and all the energy out of my body. She was a human pinprick, popping all the colorful balloons in life and deflating them. After listening, praying, and asking for His love for her, I gave her my diagnosis. I told her that she had a "terminal case of negativity."

She was thrilled to have been given a diagnosis. I suggested that upon her return home, she confide in a trusted friend her diagnosis and give that friend permission to hold her accountable. I proposed that this friend, whenever possible, privately correct her. In public settings, the friend could simply pull on her earlobe to signal her to stop whenever she began a negative rant. By the end of our time together, she left in much better spirits.

Two weeks later she called back with an update. She was excited to tell me she had been cured. She was proud that she was no longer terminally negative and to her amazement was generally happy most of the time. She confirmed that she'd followed through and recruited an accountability partner. "But," she hesitated, "my friend has developed a major problem. Her earlobe is now about a foot long!" What a testimony to the Lord's goodness that this negative person turned out to have such a terrific sense of humor. Thank You, Lord!

If your supplicant tends to focus on the negative issues of life, I strongly suggest that you ask them what they hope to achieve. "Seek first his kingdom" (Matthew 6:33) should become their new go-to verse. Help them learn to default to the Creator of positive thinking—our Lord and Savior, Jesus Christ!

Sin

Of course sin is a block to healing. Sin is a block to every good and perfect gift that our God destined for us. So labeling sin as a block to healing is of no surprise, but it is of great consequence to us. When reading the Scripture, whenever Jesus healed or cured someone, He often said, "Your sins are forgiven" (Matthew 9:2; Mark 2:5, 9; Luke 5:20 and 7:48). Jesus is also known to have cautioned those He healed to sin no more.

What does that tell us? I think it alerts us to a clear and direct correlation between sin and sickness. When we sin, we open ourselves up to the forces of evil that surround us every day, through which sickness can access us. We are told in James 5:16: "Therefore confess your sins to each other and pray for each other so that you may be healed." Hmmm . . . we know that whenever there is a "therefore," it is there for a reason. It suggests that what follows is a conclusion to whatever preceded it. So, let's look back at James 5:15: "And the prayer offered in faith will make the sick person well; the Lord will raise them up. If they have sinned, they will be forgiven."

This is not rocket science. Healing incorporates the forgiveness of sins. When we sin, we block our healing. To unblock, or allow healing to flow into our bodies, minds, and spirits, we are to confess our sins and pray in faith to be forgiven and healed. Isn't it lovely that when we are healed from a disease or other malady our sins are forgiven? Healing is more than a "pretty face." It moves to the marrow and encompasses our entire beings. Healed, we are clean slates.

I have experienced the ire of supplicants who, having felt healed for a few days following prayer, call me back to grumble that their healing "effect" has worn off and they're unwell again. It is then that I ask about their sinful habits. Immediately, the door of communication slams shut. Many people shut down, refusing confession. Others, to my great joy, willingly confess. I have heard confessions of worshipping idols and even false gods. I am convinced that our sins block healing.

The antidote is our willingness to confess our sins, seek absolution, and pray we are healed. Help your supplicants confess their sins, pray for each other, receive absolution, and be set free from past and present sins.

Generational Blocks

Some years ago, I was in Rutland, Vermont, at an annual Fishnet Conference hosted by the Christian Healing Ministry and the MacNutts. There were more than five hundred at the gathering. Late in the day Francis, Judith, and I were praying for those desiring prayer. A woman approached me. As she was walking toward me, I had a vision. I saw a closet door open. There stood a white-boned skeleton with his hands on his hips, smiling. I heard the skeleton say, "Thank you, I've been waiting for years to be set free." To my astonishment the skeleton then ran off. I gently shared what I had seen with the woman, and she was ecstatic—over the moon delighted. She simply said, "You don't need to pray for me. The Lord has already taken care of the issue." After hugging me she went on her way with a huge smile on her face.

Several weeks after returning home, I got a package in the mail. It contained a small wooden box with a latch on it. Upon opening the latch, a skeleton popped out hanging on a clothes rail alongside tiny articles of clothing on small hangers. The accompanying note read, "I've been set free, thank you." As I write this now, it still brings a smile to my face. Who other than Jesus would know the specific felt needs of that woman who came for prayer in Vermont? In the blink of an eye, after He gave me the vision of a skeleton, she was set free from the sins of her father and mother and all the other relatives in her family line. Unbeknown to her, the blocks that had kept her from receiving God's love and healing were historically linked to her ancestral line. Without heroics on her part, or mine, the Lord broke through and expedited her healing.

As we saw earlier, the generational blocks to healing may be intricately entwined with other blocks to healing. As we rethink every block I have written about, we could make a case that our ancestral lines may be enmeshed in those blocks. Fortunately, more and more healing ministries around the globe are reckoning with generational blocks to healing. It is worth our effort to have our supplicants think long and hard about their families of origin. Though they may not know specifics or even the names of some family members, they might have heard rumors and stories about uncle so-and-so, or their mother's grandpa, or a spinster great-aunt. They must ask the Lord to show them what lies beneath, then name and repent of anything that is holding them hostage.

Rejection

I have met many people who have been emotionally, physically, or spiritually abused. They have suffered serious trauma or repeated abuse that has led them to conclude that they are castoffs—disposable and unlovable. Access to healing is blocked by their overwhelming sense of rejection. The intensity of their experiences with rejection is not allayed by presenting the truth that they've been deceived by their perpetrators' actions. To overcome the damage of rejection, they must be confronted by the scandalous love of God in Christ Jesus.

A woman came to meet with me and shared her terrible and tragic life. As I shared previously, though I had never met her before, she was hostile and combative. I wondered what I might have done to upset her. Her anger seemed to be directed at me, and I was perplexed as to why. While she continued with her story, it became clear that she was transferring her personal history of rejection to me. As she went on, a picture formed in my mind of a long list of people who had rejected her. Each name on that list had a check mark next to it, except my name at the bottom, which had no check against it yet!

Suddenly, I recognized that God was downloading His insight about this woman before me. I told her, firmly, that I would not allow her to reject me. I let her know I knew that because her life was filled with rejection she anticipated I would also reject her. I explained that in her attempt to have an upper hand in our meeting, she had purposed herself to reject me before I could reject her. This, of course, was a divine revelation, as I am simply not that smart or insightful. However, it was beyond exciting to know that God loved her so much that He imparted His knowledge about her to me.

How was I going to handle this? Well, I thought a good place to start would be with Jesus Christ, who said, "I will never leave you or reject you." If Jesus could deliver on that, I knew He could use me to do that also. I assured her that whatever she said or did to me I would not reject her. I helped her understand what she was doing and why. I explained that Jesus, though subjected to death upon a cross, never rejected anyone. I delivered Jesus to her and helped her allow Him to confront her wounds and heal them. We slowly dealt with all the rejection in her life, and Jesus replaced it with His truth and set her free. Like an artichoke peeled to reveal its sweet and sumptuous heart, this woman's layers of pain were peeled back to expose a heart resuscitated by the love of Christ. She was visibly transformed. I watched God work in the heart of this woman to make her willing to receive Him. Thanks be to God!

Here is a prayer you may ask your supplicants to pray to begin their healing journey:

Jesus, I suffer from doubt, anxiety, and fear. I no longer want to live my life in this oppression. Jesus, please heal me of all negativity and set me free. Help me to become the person You designed me to be. Jesus, I can no longer carry the weight of my burdens, but I trust You can. Please help me to place everything at the foot of Your cross and allow me to leave it there. I want to know You and, through You, to see myself the way You see me. I forgive everyone who taught me to feel defeat in the face of doubt, anxiety, and fear. I forgive myself for allowing my life and my emotions to be out of Your control. Thank You, God, for setting this captive free. I love You, Jesus, and give You all the glory. Amen.

UNANSWERED PRAYER

He could not do any miracles there, except lay
his hands on a few sick people and heal them.
—Mark 6:5

The mystery of how God responds to our prayers for healing of others is often difficult to solve. The answers to our prayers may be yes, no, or later. But when we pray for healing, we can be assured that every person is healed, though not all are totally cured. It is all such a mystery, except this part: something always happens when we pray. I have prayed for some precious souls who received the ultimate healing and have passed on to glory. There was no doubt in my mind or theirs that they were healed. I have seen progressive healing as well as immediate, instantaneous healing. Some folks have had symptoms lessened and their need for medications reduced. Years after praying, I have also been privileged to witness the dramatic changes in the lives of some supplicants that have abundantly blessed them and their loved ones. Though I occasionally hear some complain that the process of healing is so slow, I can help them remember how far they have come as we look back together. Many have said thank you to God while many others have not, even though they received healing.

In our culture of consumerism in the United States, we have come to expect instant gratification, instant healing, and instantly answered prayer. Though that certainly can happen—and often does—it is not always that way. Sometimes there are only subtle changes for the better, often unnoticed by the supplicant though entirely evident to others, particularly their caregivers.

Oswald Chambers, a Scottish Baptist evangelist and teacher, left a treasure trove of teachings before he died in 1917 at the age of forty-three. Posthumously, his widow transcribed all his lectures and messages, and published thirty books or articles including *My Utmost for His Highest*, from which this excerpt is quoted:

> Our thinking about prayer, whether right or wrong, is based on our own mental conception of it. The correct concept is to think of prayer as the breath in our lungs and the blood from our hearts. Our blood flows and our breathing continues "without ceasing"; we are not even conscious of it, but it never stops. . . . Prayer is not an exercise, it is the life of the saints. . . .
>
> Jesus never mentioned unanswered prayer. He had the certainty of knowing that prayer is always answered. . . . Jesus said, "Everyone who asks receives" (Matthew 7:8). Yet we say, "But . . . but . . ." God answers prayer in the best way— not just sometimes, but every time . . ."[1]

While we're at it, let's look at one other excerpt from *My Utmost for His Highest*:

> Jesus said that because of His name God will recognize and respond to our prayers. What a great challenge and invitation—to pray in His name! Through the resurrection and ascension power of Jesus, and through the Holy Spirit He has sent, we can be lifted into such a relationship. Once in that wonderful position, having been placed there by Jesus Christ, we can pray to God in Jesus' name—in His

nature. This is a gift granted to us through the Holy Spirit, and Jesus said, ". . . whatever you ask the Father in My name He will give you."[2]

Nothing answers our questions better than God's Word. Does God ever fail to answer the prayers of those who put their trust in Him? No, never! Though Chambers spoke those words more than a hundred years ago, his answer still rings true. That's because Jesus Christ is the same today as He was yesterday and will be tomorrow (Hebrews 13:8). One of my earliest mentors, the Rev. Canon Jim Glennon, agreed with Chambers that God always answers the prayers of those who seek Him in earnest. Canon Glennon loved to quote a passage from the Bible that was near and dear to his heart. Sadly, I don't hear many healing prayer ministers referencing these verses today.

> He [Jesus] also said, "This is what the kingdom of God is like. A man scatters seed on the ground. Night and day, whether he sleeps or gets up, the seed sprouts and grows, though he does not know how. All by itself the soil produces grain—first the stalk, then the head, then the full kernel in the head. As soon as the grain is ripe, he puts the sickle to it, because the harvest has come." (Mark 4:26–29)

I can hear the booming voice of the imposing presence of Canon Glennon with his Aussie accent reading this passage aloud. Consider that for both Glennon and myself, relating this scripture in the context of healing is primary and uppermost to all other possible meanings. As I unpack this, remember that my focus—and now yours—should be purposefully trying to better understand various aspects of healing prayer and how God answers.

We read, definitively, that this passage is all about God and His work: "He [Jesus] also said, 'This is what the kingdom of God is like. A man scatters seed on the ground'" (Mark 4:26). Before moving on to verse 27, we are reminded that before the plant can be seen, it must put down roots into the soil to help it stand up. In healing, this communicates that there is some groundwork that God wants to be accomplished before we see evidence of the new plant emerging. This verse is also the basis of my caveat to healing prayer ministers: "Don't pull up roots!"

Verse 27 says, "Night and day, whether he sleeps or gets up, the seed sprouts and grows, though he does not know how." This verse reinforces that it is only God who is able to effect change (healing) on His children. The man who scattered the seed on the field went to bed and whether he was awake, overseeing the field, or fast asleep, leaving it idle, the seed grows, and the man has not a clue how.

In verse 28 we read, "All by itself the soil produces grain—first the stalk, then the head, then the full kernel in the head." Slam dunk! "All by itself . . ." via God's help by providing for sun, rain, and warmth, the seed produces grain—and gradually, ever so steadily, the new plant puts down its roots and breaks through the ground to take its stand above ground. That's believable! Yes, indeed! We know that a seed needs water, light, and heat to grow—all provided by God. We also know that healing requires faith, love, forgiveness, and confession—all provided by God. If we healing ministers will listen, love, and pray, out of our belief in Him, healing will follow.

Verse 29 concludes, "As soon as the grain is ripe, he puts the sickle to it, because the harvest has come." In other words, we healing ministers, having scattered seed and done the groundwork that the Lord has directed, can close our faith-filled prayers "in the name of Jesus!" and the harvest of God's healing work, through us as His vessels, will be made evident to all.

Please enjoy taking another look at this passage in *The Message*:

Then Jesus said, "God's kingdom is like seed thrown on a field by a man who then goes to bed and forgets about it. The seed sprouts and grows—he has no idea how it happens. The earth does it all without his help: first a green stem of grass, then a bud, then the ripened grain. When the grain is fully formed, he reaps—harvest time!

Canon Glennon loved this passage because it aptly describes our role in healing. Though we are privileged to be facilitators of God's provisions for healing, He alone heals. Of course, there may be times when we may not appreciate His answer or His timing, but He never fails to answer those who believe in Him and seek Him. God is still in the business of answering prayer and healing His children—of this I have no doubt.

Now that we have documented that God is faithful to those who have faith in Him, we need to examine the circumstances under which our God may not hear our prayers, much less answer them. This is difficult to accept, because it seems to contradict His nature. But it is entirely consistent. Throughout this book I've shared that there is always His part, our part, and our supplicant's part. It is possible when we or our supplicant are not doing our part, that He may not do His. If either of us is not in a personal relationship with Him; if we have not accepted Him as our Lord and Savior; if we are "acting out" against Him, then He may not be inclined to answer us when we call upon Him for healing.

Here are some of the circumstances that can cause God to close His ears to our petitions for His grace, mercy, provision, or healing:

We do not ask. "You do not have, because you do not ask God" (James 4:2).

We ask with wrong motives. "When you ask, you do not receive, because you ask with wrong motives, that you may spend what you get on your pleasures" (James 4:3).

We can be out of the will of God by being covetous. "Son of man, these men have set up idols in their hearts and put wicked stumbling blocks before their faces. Should I let them inquire of me at all?" (Ezekiel 14:3).

Injustice. "When you spread out your hands in prayer, I hide my eyes from you; even when you offer many prayers, I am not listening. . . . Learn to do right; seek justice. Defend the oppressed" (Isaiah 1:15, 17).

Unbelief. "But when you ask, you must believe and not doubt, because the one who doubts is like a wave of the sea, blown and tossed by the wind. That person should not expect to receive anything from the Lord" (James 1:6–7).

Sin (in supplicants or prayer ministers). "But your iniquities have separated you from your God; your sins have hidden his face from you, so that he will not hear" (Isaiah 59:2).

Selfishness. "Whoever shuts their ears to the cry of the poor will also cry out and not be answered" (Proverbs 21:13).

Rebellion. "They made their hearts as hard as flint and would not listen. . . . 'When I called, they did not listen; so when they called, I would not listen,' says the Lord Almighty" (Zechariah 7:12–13).

Pride. "Israel's arrogance testifies against them. . . . When they . . . seek the Lord, they will not find him; he has withdrawn himself from them" (Hosea 5:5–6).

Disharmony. "Husbands, in the same way be considerate as you live with your wives . . . so that nothing will hinder your prayers" (1 Peter 3:7).

As you ponder God's disclaimers of His provision and protection, please meditate on the many scriptures that exhort us to "fear the Lord your God." Take a look now at Deuteronomy 10:12: "What does the Lord your God ask of you but to fear the Lord your God, to walk in obedience to him, to love him, to serve the Lord your God with all your heart and with all your soul." God tells us to fear Him, because

He knows that we idolize whatever we fear. If we are afraid of our boss, our fear will cause our boss to loom greater than our God. If we fear God, we will keep a laser focus on Him and will enjoy an ongoing, loving relationship with Him. When we move away from Him and posture ourselves out of His grasp, we become estranged from Him.

The above list of ten circumstances is merely representative of how we can become estranged from Him even in the midst of our healing ministry. There are other circumstances, of course. Each jeopardizes our relationship with God and must be remedied before we can be restored to Him and continue with our calling. Confession and repentance are the keys to bridging any gap between Him and us. The antidote to overcoming that which threatens God's willingness to hear and answer our prayers, is found in the following passages:

> Whoever conceals their sins does not prosper, but the one who confesses and renounces them finds mercy. (Proverbs 28:13)

> Then I acknowledged my sin to You and did not cover up my iniquity. I said, "I will confess my transgressions to the LORD." And you forgave the guilt of my sin. (Psalm 32:5)

> Therefore confess your sins to each other and pray for each other so that you may be healed. The prayer of a righteous person is powerful and effective. (James 5:16)

How do we reconcile His potential answers of yes, no, or later? We simply remember who He truly is and how scandalously He loves those who have put their trust in Him. Recalling His nature and trusting that no one could ever know us better or love us more, we can patiently wait, in faith and with expectancy, for His answer to arrive on time and flawlessly appropriate. If healing prayer ministers doubt this truth in any way, our supplicants may also!

Twelve Components of Healing Prayer

For more than a quarter of a century of being available to the Lord in healing ministry, I have been able to identify twelve major components of healing prayer:

1. Christian healing is all about releasing disease and dis-ease in the name of Jesus Christ.

2. Christian healing is all about love.

3. When we pray, something always happens.

4. We need to approach healing ministry with an attitude of gratitude. It was St. Chrysostom who said, "Give thanks in all things." And we also find in 1 Thessalonians 5:16–18: "Rejoice always, pray continually, give thanks in all circumstances; for this is God's will for you in Christ Jesus."

5. Everyone is healed, but not everyone is "cured."

6. Christian healing requires an open vessel through which the Lord can work.

7. Healing prayer is a mystery.

8. Listen, love, and pray.

9. Christian healing is about faith working through love (but not necessarily the faith of the supplicant). "The only thing that counts is faith expressing itself through love" (Galatians 5:6).

10. Healing is answered prayer. "Pray for each other so that you may be healed" (James 5:16).

11. God does give gifts to us, indeed His greater gifts. "Now to each one the manifestation of the Spirit is given for the common good. . . . to another gifts of healing by that one Spirit" (1 Corinthians 12:7, 9).

12. We can be confident we are to pray for another's healing when He sends us. "And he sent them out to proclaim the kingdom of God and to heal the sick" (Luke 9:2).

CHURCH

Heal the sick, raise the dead, cleanse
those who have leprosy, drive out demons.
Freely you have received; freely give.
—Matthew 10:8

Many years ago, my now deceased father, the Rev. David Mumford, an Anglican priest, was in a bookstore in London. A woman came into the shop and with a very loud and demanding voice queried all the patrons in the shop, "Does anyone know anything about healing?" My father cautiously approached the woman and introduced himself. She told my dad that her daughter was sick and she was hoping to find a book that would help her. My father took her to the healing section in the store, and among the books he showed her were *Healing*, written by Francis MacNutt, and *Dancer Off Her Feet*, written by Julie Mumford Sheldon, my sister. He shared about the ministry of his daughter, an author in the UK, and of his son (me, not yet published) in the US, as well as the ministry of Francis MacNutt, a former Roman Catholic priest. He then prayed with her for the healing of her daughter.

As it happened Francis MacNutt was soon to lead a healing conference for Presbyterian pastors in Edinburgh, Scotland. This woman took a train from London to Edinburgh to meet Francis.

The healing service at St. Cuthbert's Presbyterian Church drew four hundred people and lasted until 2:30 a.m. Before it ended, dozens of Presbyterian ministers had been baptized in the Holy Spirit.

The woman my father had prayed for shared the testimony of her daughter's healing in front of four hundred Scottish pastors. She explained how she had stormed into a London bookshop and demanded to know about healing. She told how my father had recommended Francis MacNutt's book and how, after reading that book, she applied what she had learned and prayed for her daughter, who was subsequently healed. She had traveled to Edinburgh to say thank you to Francis and to the Lord for His faithfulness.

Odd, isn't it? A desperate mother searched out a bookstore—not a church—to learn about healing. The tragedy is that though her story is now many years old, nothing much has changed. Healing services and healing ministries remain rare occurrences within the Christian church and its many denominations. It boggles my mind why every church is not a hospital for those seeking Christ's healing. We are apparently afraid to carry out the command of Jesus to His disciples (and to us!): "When Jesus had called the Twelve together, he gave them power and authority to drive out all demons and to cure diseases, and he sent them out to proclaim the kingdom of God and to heal the sick. . . . So they set out and went from village to village, proclaiming the good news and healing people everywhere" (Luke 9:1–2, 6).

As one who regularly teaches, preaches, and ministers in Christ's healing gifts, I find it nonsensical that this woman went to a bookstore to learn about the living God. It is not too far a stretch to think that God is, Himself, concerned about His church's lack of healing, since He arranged for my father to minister to the cry of that mother's heart. So why aren't churches offering healing prayer today? Let's reacquaint ourselves with the Lord's "marching orders" found in James 5:13–16:

> Is anyone among you in trouble? Let them pray. Is anyone happy?
> Let them sing songs of praise. Is anyone among you sick? Let them

call the elders of the church to pray over them and anoint them with oil in the name of the Lord. And the prayer offered in faith will make the sick person well; the Lord will raise them up. If they have sinned, they will be forgiven. Therefore confess your sins to each other and pray for each other so that you may be healed. The prayer of a righteous person is powerful and effective.

Despite such clarity in the Scriptures, the modern church is virtually silent on the healing gifts of Jesus Christ. From my vantage point, there are too few healing ministries and healing services available to meet the needs of Christ's followers. We certainly can agree that the church is no longer operating under the same understanding as the early church—that the sick would be able to ask the elders, of any and every church, to pray for them to be made well. I do know that there is no lack of demand among Christians for healing. So how do we get churches to offer more healing services and healing ministries? We must plant and grow them. But to do so, we must be mindful of several factors:

The Basics

1. Would a healing service or healing ministry, in your church or neighborhood, be redundant? Do other nearby churches offer healing? Perhaps you could begin attending their services regularly and volunteer to work with them, gaining valuable experience and wisdom as you pray through your desire to plant a ministry in your home church.

2. Do you have spiritual maturity? Workers in any church ministry must learn that it is not about them. Spiritually mature believers understand that there is nothing in, or about, us that adds to what the Lord does through us. In other words, to serve in a healing ministry is a privilege and requires us to get out

of God's way. It's not about us—it is all about Him! The only "star" in the ministry of healing is Jesus Christ!

3. Do you have like-minded fellow church members? Are there others in your church who share your desire to launch a regular healing service or healing ministry? You will definitely need more than yourself to get started. We know that God sends us out, in the least, in twos. Pray and ask the Lord to show you who the potential "others" are in your church. You can use this checklist:

 – Are they spiritually mature?
 – Do they nurture a deep, abiding personal love relationship with Jesus?
 – Do they believe that Jesus still heals today? Do they have a personal story to that effect?
 – Do they understand how vital it is to have absolute confidentiality?
 – Are they "teachable," or do they resist learning from others?
 – Are they humble? Are they aware that the more they get out of God's way, the more useful they become?
 – Do they respect authority, particularly the authority of their church leadership?

Getting Started:
1. Gather with your like-minded brothers and sisters in Christ for study and discernment. Pray together for discernment about planting a healing ministry, asking the Lord to show each of you whether He is inspiring you to do this.
2. Find a book to study together. Meet weekly for at least twelve weeks as you work your way through a book study and cleave as a team. Everyone must grow to trust one another and freely share their thoughts, fears, doubts, and so forth. Don't use

any book that demands you only use its manual or method of healing. Look to the Bible as your manual and Jesus Christ as your model. Suggested books: *This Is Where Your Healing Begins* (by me); *Healing* and *The Nearly Perfect Crime*, both by Francis MacNutt; or *Your Healing Is Within You*, by the Rev. Canon Jim Glennon.

3. As your team is knit together, meet for twelve more weeks and pray a) for one another's needs, b) for your church leadership, and c) for others in your church who are publicly known to be sick (not confidential needs). This is a discipline in maintaining confidentiality. Even if one of your team was told, privately, of a need—unless it was shared with all of you, it is not to be included in your group prayer meetings.

Important Considerations and Next Steps:

1. Does your church leadership believe in the healing gifts of Jesus Christ?

2. Does your church leadership have an expectancy of God to answer their prayers?

3. Does your church leadership pursue and nurture lay involvement in ministry?

4. Is there a protocol to follow within your church on how to launch new ministries?

5. Ask someone within your study and discernment group to write a brief overview of your group's vision for a healing ministry within your church.

6. Ask that no more than two members of your study and discernment group present your vision in a meeting with your senior pastor or rector. In this meeting, be sure to let your pastor know that you don't want to add to his or her existing workload, but that it is important for him or her to either personally be involved in this ministry or assign associate clergy

to oversee it on his or her behalf—or, perhaps, a lay liaison might do.

7. If your pastor is open to this ministry, request that an expanded meeting be called comprised of others he or she would like to be involved in the launching of this ministry.

Please understand that these are suggestions and not hard and fast rules. Every denomination is different, and every church within a denomination is different from one another. Following the procedures unique to each church will benefit everyone as you contemplate launching a healing service or a healing ministry. Give some thought to moving slower by beginning with only a healing service. The order of service should be compatible with your church's regular services in form, while adding a direct emphasis on Christ's healing gifts and healing prayer.

There is some wisdom in limiting your launch to the introduction of healing services, because it immediately incorporates your clergy in the process. The pastor(s) of the church would lead a healing service as they do when they celebrate Sunday services. The sermon or message of a healing service would, naturally, focus on scriptures that highlight healing. The major (initial) departure from Sunday services would be the allotment of more time for healing prayer to be offered to attendees, either during the service or at the end. Your study and discernment group will likely provide the healing prayer ministers essential for that portion of your healing service.

The Healing Service

Format: Since the well-being and comfort of your church members are essential, using an order of service familiar to your church membership may be best. In time, a natural progression toward a more specific and unique order of service may evolve; but in the beginning, what is familiar to your church will help your future healing ministry take root in your church body.

Order of Service: Every church has its own liturgy, a word that simply means "a form of worship" and is synonymous with the word *service.* So even nonliturgical denominations are liturgical! As I have said, your initial order of service can closely follow your Sunday bulletin as you ease your church family into this new healing service. Simply because it is a healing service, some components in your order of service may be extraordinary. Here are a few possibilities:

- *Praise and Worship.* Though most church services include music, a healing service is replete with praise music. Finding a worship leader capable of ministering with instrumental music during quiet times and corporate worship is helpful. All sacred music, traditional or contemporary, is truly able to soothe and heal souls.
- *Scripture Readings.* The healing service may include more verses than are usually read at a regular service. Selected scriptures can be read aloud from "the front" ("altar area"); said together corporately by all in attendance; or read aloud, individually, by assigning attendees to speak from their seats. The scriptures should focus on the healing gifts of Jesus and all aspects of healing in body, mind, and spirit.
- *Homily or Message.* Like a sermon, but briefer, it is laser focused on healing. At least one Scripture verse, related to the message, should preface the homily.
- *Corporate Prayer Time.* Whether printed in a bulletin or projected on a screen, corporate prayers can be said aloud, together. These prayers may include confession, repentance, or intercessions. They might also provide a time for attendees to share, aloud or silently, the first names of those they know to be in need of healing.
- *Testimony.* Initially, you may pre-arrange one or two brief (two- to three-minute) testimonies of individuals who want to praise

God for a healing they received. These can be given following the homily, but before the laying on of hands. As the service matures, you might ask for volunteers during the service . . . but wait until you've modeled how testimonies are to be given (brief; limited details; praising God and never the one who prayed).

- *The Laying On of Hands / Healing Prayer.* This can be done within the healing service or at the end of the service. Your study and discernment group will field personnel for your healing prayer teams (of two) to offer prayer for those seeking healing for themselves (or in proxy for another). When this time of prayer is designated within the service, prayer teams respond by praying for those with raised hands, at their seats. If Communion is included in your service, before returning to their seats, attendees may seek out prayer teams at stations located in the sanctuary. When healing prayer is offered after the service ends, attendees may receive prayer by waiting at stations where prayer teams are assigned. They may leave after they have received prayer. Attendees not desiring prayer may be quietly dismissed.

- *Holy Communion.* Though it is not essential to offer Communion, you may find it to be most beneficial. Visiting attendees who rarely take Communion often find the act of receiving Communion very healing. Though including it will add time to your service, there are abbreviated rites that could greatly reduce the extra time required.

- *Unction (Anointing with Oil).* In some traditions, oil is blessed by clergy in advance and applied to the foreheads of those who receive healing prayer. This can either be done during or following Holy Communion *or* by the prayer teams after they have prayed for each person. Again, it is not essential, but is very often beneficial.

- *Announcements.* These may be shared at any point within your order of service. Your announcements will grow as your healing services take root and your church births a full healing ministry. You might include news of healing missions or speaker conferences being offered nearby, the formation of prayer groups or study groups, as well as other prayer services for: soaking prayer, generational healing, healing of memories, inner healing, deliverance, confession, the litany for the dying, and so forth.

Before I continue, this might be a good place to discuss the distinction between introducing a healing service within your church and resourcing a full-fledged healing ministry. While a healing service can meet the felt needs of service attendees by providing on-the-spot laying on of hands in prayer, a fully resourced healing ministry can offer additional healing prayer to church members, and eventually to the local community, which extend beyond the laying on of hands. In this book, I have written about inner healing ministry, the healing of memories, generational healing, and deliverance, among other topics. These are just some components of a fully functioning healing ministry that require an equipped staff of (paid or volunteer) personnel.

For the most part, a healing ministry will naturally emerge from a church's commitment to host healing services on a regular basis. As a church gets its "sea legs" in providing healing services, the next step is to move to a regular weekly or monthly healing service. If that service is only offered during daytime hours, consideration for an additional regular weekly evening service should also be seriously given. Not everyone is able to attend weekday daytime services. Word will travel fast, and your church will likely become a lighthouse for healing in the community.

Since your church began first by offering public healing services, it is my guess that your clergy and church leadership will have become increasingly supportive of this new ministry. Of no surprise to us, but perhaps to them, will be how many "visitors" to your healing service become or grow deeper as believers in Jesus Christ. Grateful to the Lord, visitors may also join your church or join your team of inspired believers who want to serve and be used to further Christ's kingdom in your community. The upside of healing is endless.

When this happens, your church will likely become the proud parent of a new healing ministry.

As you might expect, arriving at this juncture, your team of volunteers will have continued to faithfully pray with attendees at your healing services. They are the nucleus of your healing services and will resource a fully functioning healing ministry. Over time, having ministered together, your team will likely discern special spiritual gifting within it members. These gifts are bestowed upon your team members by the Holy Spirit and are distributed to those who have asked Him to be used as vessels of His healing gifts. All spiritual gifts are given for the common good. "Now to each one the manifestation of the Spirit is given for the common good" (1 Corinthians 12:7).

Since I believe that all the gifts of the Holy Spirit are essential in healing ministry, your team should pray for whatever is lacking. Among the more evident manifestations of the Spirit in healing are His gifts of faith, wisdom, prophecy, encouragement, knowledge, love, or discernment. No spiritual gift, however, is irrelevant. The Lord will faithfully pour out every spiritual resource necessary to heal His children, when those seeking Him are sincere and humble.

A viable full-service healing ministry is dependent upon well-qualified and equipped healing ministers—so, in moving forward, look for and to these identifiable qualities and characteristics in your team members who are called by Jesus to function as healing ministers:

- *Healing prayer ministers must remain open to receiving ministry.* It is important for everyone to both give and receive. Seek out this attribute in those you recruit.

- *Healing prayer ministers never graduate*; they remain "learners" forever. Yes, some are more experienced than others, but the Holy Spirit rarely does the same thing twice—so healing ministers worth their salt can never rest on their laurels! They must always learn!

- *Healing prayer ministers must draw upon their own alive, personal love relationships with Jesus and His Holy Spirit.* Vet your team members. Teaching and mentoring must be required for all, no matter how experienced. A wise priest once said, "You train seals, you teach healing ministers!" Experienced prayer ministers may simply need to be mentored in your ministry's protocols and agree to abide by them. Others may need in-depth teaching to become equipped for service. The School of Healing Prayer has DVD teachings from Christian Healing Ministry in Jacksonville, Florida, and can be a starting point in teaching (if used *in addition to* the Bible as your manual and Jesus as your model!).

- Individually, and corporately as a team, devour recommended books on healing to gain an in-depth understanding. But allow Jesus to vet what you retain from your reading.

- Encourage your clergy to preach healing from the pulpit at your healing and regular church services and to encourage believers to receive Christ's healing in body, mind, and spirit. Provide prayer teams at every church service to meet the felt needs of the people.

- Scout for medical personnel (doctors, nurses, psychologists, EMTs) who believe in Jesus and His healing gifts to give a homily or message at your weekly healing service.

- In organizing your healing teams of two persons, create opportunities for them to pray for each other and utilize them to provide prayer at church services every week.

- Send your healing prayer teams out to nursing homes, hospitals, and rehabilitative facilities to pray for those who have expressed a desire for healing.

- Be sure that your healing team regularly listens, loves, and prays for one another and becomes equipped to listen, love, and pray for those who seek healing in your services.
- Jump-start the establishment of a full-fledged healing ministry by inviting well-respected clergy or laity to speak at one-day workshops or multiple-day conferences or missions.
- Have your team lead a Sunday school class where church members can learn more about the healing gifts of Jesus Christ, particularly that He still heals today.
- Have your healing team members volunteer to take your church's (or denomination's) safety course to protect against sexual harassment and abuse.
- When it seems right to the Holy Spirit, to church leadership, and to your healing team, begin offering individual prayer appointments to your church members first. Appointments will be made with your prayer teams, for those in need of inner healing, deliverance, confession, the healing of memories, and so forth.
- Be an encourager and begin to empower and commission more and more laypeople to join your team of learners. Defend against any pride, exclusivity, or airs of superiority within the launching prayer team. All are only learners. Others, who God calls, may join your team later and may run circles around even your most experienced team members. It is only Christ, in us, who will provide healing. Don't ever forget that!
- James 2:22 reminds us that our faith is known by its fruit: "You see that his faith and his actions were working together, and his faith was made complete by what he did."

The road to launching a healing ministry will not be easy, but every experience is essential and God-ordained if your team and your church are committed to glorifying God in your healing services. But there *will* be bumps in the road ahead. Here are important caveats to be aware of:

- The motivations for launching a healing service and, ultimately, a healing ministry cannot be for the purposes of growing your church membership. It is repugnant to use Jesus' spiritual gifts to advance your church's station in the community. I strongly caution you to root out any hint of this misguided way of thinking.
- Unless your pastor, vicar, rector, or presbyter is on board with healing, there can be no healing service or healing ministry in your church, for good reason. As you wait upon the Lord to make a way, seek out local churches where you can get involved in Christian healing until your home church is ready.
- The number of attendees at your healing service is irrelevant. Never ascribe the adjective *successful* to any ministry of Jesus Christ, especially not to healing. Don't keep track of how many people attend your services. You'll know that all is well when the Lord begins to send His children to you on a regular basis. Resist, also, any church leadership effort to track matters of accounting regarding healing. If only one person shows up, you have been obedient.
- Give careful thought before establishing an "offering segment" in your order of service. Yes, there are costs, but blessings *will* follow your church's selfless generosity. Don't box out God's desire to creatively bless you in unexpected ways. It is okay, of course, to put out a basket at the entrance or exit of your sanctuary, simply labeled "Offerings."
- You'll likely hear some church members comment: "We've never done *this* before!" Be tenacious in your efforts to be kind and compassionate and be ready to give a godly answer to those who may criticize your efforts. Pray they'll come for healing.

- Confidentiality. When anyone asks for prayer, do not repeat the request or substance of your prayers to anyone else. Since you'll always pray in teams of two, unless you are troubled about the process (only) of the prayers you experienced, the substance of your prayers should not be discussed later. Even if the person you prayed for is a friend, do not contact them and ask, "How are you doing?" That is tea and sympathy, not godly prayer. Christ alone knows. It's better to err on the side of appearing uncaring than to flag a prayer concern again. Ask God to remove from you the remembrance of the *substance* of your prayers for others.
- Before praying for others with the laying on of hands, encourage any clergy present to pray for the prayer team members' safety, obedience to God, and wisdom.
- Following prayer for others, pray for your partner and ask your partner to pray for you that God will not allow anything that is not of Him to remain with either of you. Ask Jesus to set you totally free of anything that might trouble you later.

If you are reading this and are ordained clergy, with Jesus' heart for healing, I want to encourage you to boldly step out and share your beliefs with your congregants or parishioners, by preaching the kingdom of God and the healing gifts of Jesus Christ (Luke 9:2). One of two things will likely happen: 1) A person you pray for may die. 2) A person you pray for may be healed or cured. In any event, the responsibility for the result of your prayers is God's alone. When you are obedient to Him in faith and believe that He is not only willing to heal but able, the result of your prayers is of concern to no one other than Him and to the person for whom you have prayed.

In stretching out your hands to heal others in Christ's name, you will not always know whether a person has faith and a personal relationship with Christ Jesus. You will not always know whether a person even wants to be made well. You will not always know the areas in a person's life in need of healing (relationships, bitterness, unforgiveness, and so forth). You will not always know if people have forgiven themselves. You will not always know all that is blocking a person from receiving healing. But you do know Jesus! And you do know that He heals. You also know that Christ knows better than you the persons for whom you pray, and He loves them more than anyone else.

Pastors, I am exhorting you to trust God, the one who knows you best and loves you most, the one who called you to ordination. Trust Him to be faithful and demonstrate His lovingkindness to all those you will lift upon the stretchers of your prayers, to Him.

I sold my business in 1995 and in the same year established a healing retreat center called the Oratory of the Little Way of St. Therese of Lisieux in Gaylordsville, Connecticut. At that time, I attended St. John's Church, in New Milford, where a beloved female parishioner had taken ill. My spirit, however, was utterly convinced that this woman would be healed and cured. After all, I had sold everything and was dedicating my life to Jesus' healing ministry. When she ultimately died, I was crushed. It was a very tough start to full-time healing ministry; but I persevered with my Royal Marine "commando" spirit, and with His Holy Spirit, I pressed on, as Philippians 3:12 encourages us: "Not that I have already obtained all this, or have already arrived at my goal, but I press on to take hold of that for which Christ Jesus took hold of me."

So here I am today, still absorbed 365 days a year in ministry and currently writing this book in an effort to inspire others to join me in Jesus' work. When I began in the 1990s, I wasn't yet ordained. Point of fact, I did not seek ordination to be used in healing ministry—as a layperson, I ministered healing prayer to others just as much then as now! No, I was specifically called to ordination to help Jesus expand healing ministry in the modern church. Our "creds," for the most part, are rubbish and irrelevant to God in His ministry. However, in certain instances, as in my case, He may desire to formalize your role in the fulfillment of His call.

My ongoing healing work is currently an extension of my own ministry, By His Wounds, Inc., which is now located in Virginia Beach, Virginia. The prayer team that supports this ministry meets monthly for prayer, teaching, practice, updates, concerns, debriefing, and case studies. Our prayer team is a truly loving and caring community with like-minded believers. My prayer is that in reading this book you will hear God's voice call you to gather with others in your home church and plant a ministry that brings glory to the Lord Jesus Christ and His healing gifts.

I want to encourage you to get out of your comfort zone! You do know, I hope, that it is a clergyperson's job to comfort the afflicted and to afflict the comfortable. Yep! Clergy are to hatch 'em, match 'em, patch 'em, and dispatch 'em! We do whatever it takes to get Christ's bride ready. If you are anything like me, you have a passion and hope to hear Jesus say to you, on your first day in heaven: "Well done, good and faithful friend!"

Looking for the bottom line? Here it is:

Stretch out your hand to heal and perform signs and wonders through the name of your holy servant Jesus. (Acts 4:30)

And he sent them out to proclaim the kingdom of God and to heal the sick. . . . So they set out and went from village to village, proclaiming the good news and healing people everywhere. (Luke 9:2, 6)

Now go in God's peace to love and serve the Lord!

Part Three

EMOTIONS
NEEDING HEALING

DEPRESSION

A cheerful heart is good medicine,
but a crushed spirit dries up the bones.
—Proverbs 17:22

Two words spoken to me by my mentor, Dr. Francis MacNutt, totally changed my life. I was seeking his counsel when he advised me to "have fun." Because of my deepest respect for him, his words greatly impacted my life. "Have fun."

Agnes Sanford (credited for shaping Christian healing ministry as we know it today), Sir Winston Churchill, President Abraham Lincoln, and actor Robin Williams are just a few of the famous people who suffered from depression. Churchill even had a pet name for it, "The Black Dog." Depression is pervasive and indiscriminate in whomever it afflicts.

How do we safely navigate the landmines of depression? Yes, there are medications available to help alleviate its impact on us. And after praying for God's blessings on any and all medications before we take them, they can be effective. But at best they are only a Band-Aid if the underlying causes are not resolved. There are nearly as many reasons for depression as there are antidepressants. There are, however, a few contributing factors that are frequently suspected. Is depression learned from a family member? Is depression a generational issue? Is its origin genetic? Can it be induced by circumstances or situations in life? Can depression become habit forming?

My response would be yes to all the above.

Depression strikes whoever . . . whenever; but it is especially virulent in the winter. In the healing ministry we are most apt to have increased numbers of prayer appointments with supplicants during the winter months. During those appointments, however, we can unpack a depressant's history and expose the root . . . chase off and put down Churchill's "Black Dog," by setting that captive free.

A quick check of Merriam-Webster.com provided this definition of *depression*, along with some of its synonyms:

---

1. :an act of depressing or a state of being depressed: such as (1): a state of feeling sad: dejection, anger, anxiety, and depression (2): a mood disorder marked by sadness, inactivity, difficulty in thinking and concentration, a significant increase or decrease in appetite and time spent sleeping, feelings of dejection and hopelessness, and sometimes suicidal tendencies . . .

Synonyms of *Depression*

blues, dejection, desolation . . . despondence . . . disconsolateness, dispiritedness, doldrums, dolefulness, downheartedness, dreariness, dumps, forlornness, gloom . . . glumness, heartsickness, joylessness, melancholy, miserableness, mopes, mournfulness, oppression, sadness, sorrowfulness, unhappiness.

In 1978 I suffered badly from clinical depression after I received news that four of my recruits had died. As their drill instructor, I went into such a tailspin that I could not talk for a week and proceeded to stutter for six months thereafter. During that time, my mind would go to a very dark, damp, smelly place—a "Black Dog" place. I could get there so very fast! While there I would second-guess myself as to what more I could have, should have, would have done in training those lads that may have saved them. If I could have thought rationally, I would have known that their deaths were not my fault; but this depression kept me from thinking clearly. It was hell on earth, and even the prescribed medications did not work.

I was finally set free when I invited angels to go into my "Black Dog" familiar place and overpower the darkness. As I look back today, I have no idea why suicide did not enter my mind. Perhaps it is because the depression was accompanied by such low energy that I could not muster a desire, much less a plan, to do it. I now know, unmistakably, that survivors' guilt and depression had a choke hold on me. Everything in my life was distorted. I was blinded by darkness. I could not find a ray of hope. *Where are You, God?* I often asked.

Words from Job 30:24–31 in *The Message* resonate with me now— they are a brilliant description of depression:

What did I do to deserve this? Did I ever hit anyone who was calling for help? Haven't I wept for those who live a hard life, been heartsick over the lot of the poor? But where did it get me? I expected good but evil showed up. I looked for light but darkness fell. My stomach's in a constant churning, never settles down. Each day confronts me with more suffering. I walk under a black cloud. The sun is gone. I stand in the congregation and protest. I howl with the jackals, I hoot with the owls. I'm black-and-blue all over, burning up with fever. My fiddle plays nothing but the blues; my mouth harp wails laments.

Then one day, in a dream, I invited a "clean-up crew" into that dark space in my mind. The crew was made up of angels. They brought shovels, brooms, and wheelbarrows and carried away the garbage. They even pulled up the carpet, exposing a lot of "stuff" hidden underneath. It was such a mess. All the garbage that had been stored in my brain was causing my brain to emotionally rot.

In my dream, there was a cute designer angel who came with a note pad and totally redesigned the once dark space. Builder angels came and installed a palladium window and a huge flat screen TV, along with a rather nice "decliner." (I used to call them recliners . . . not so much now!) My familiar go-to dark place was demolished and was rebuilt from the ground up. The new go-to place was a modern, brightly lit man cave filled with great joy. Despite my curiosity and various attempts to access that dark, old place, it vanished, as did the burden of depression. I could no longer blame myself for the deaths of those lads because rational, sane thinking (without self-condemnation) had been restored.

The Lord showed me His presence as I emerged from that dark place. In this vision I noticed a big, black eight-ball and a ridiculously lengthy pipe that ran deep into the earth . . . deep into hell. I watched as a lever released the black eight-ball, which followed the path of a rail track affixed to the pipe. I watched as the ball stayed its course deep into the earth. As it descended it traveled faster and faster until it looked to be out of control, disappearing into the abyss. I felt ill, sick to my stomach. I was at the proverbial end of my rope.

Then I saw the hand of Jesus Christ appear near the bottom end of the pipe. With one hand He stopped the ball from spiraling out of control. It brought me great relief. Thereafter, each time I felt depressed and attempted to return to this hellish black abyss in my mind, I would see the hand of Jesus reaching closer and closer to the lever responsible for releasing the eight-ball! Then one glorious day, I saw His hand on the lever as He stopped the action completely. From that time forward, He never again let me go into that place of darkness. I was set free!

Many years later, on August 5, 2010, a hellacious mining accident occurred in Chile. For two months, thirty-three miners were trapped twenty-three hundred feet below the earth's surface. What a tragedy it was. Television news played footage of an endless tube being drilled through rock into the earth. I was suddenly reminded of the rod in my dream. One by one the surviving miners were pulled up to safety via that tube.

Since October 2009, when I survived a nearly terminal case of the swine flu (H1N1), my lungs have been greatly compromised. As I watched those miners emerge from the bowels of the earth, I could well imagine how incredible it must have been for them to breathe their first fresh air in two months! That is the freedom the Lord blessed me with when He delivered me from depression. It was as though I was able to breathe deeply after having held my breath for the duration of the depression.

I was eventually able to "proof test" my miraculous healing later, following a time when someone very close to me perpetrated a diabolical act of betrayal. I previously had complete confidence in this person who made a deliberate and calculating attempt to hijack my position in ministry. Every button was pushed as my world crashed in on me after I discovered this nefarious plot. I slipped away to the chapel on the property where I was living at that time and tried to return to the old familiar dark place in my mind. I so wanted to wallow in that hellish place again while I suffered gut-wrenching pain and grief. I just wanted to go back—deep into that place . . . I deserved it, I needed it. As Proverbs 26:11 cautions, "As a dog returns to its vomit, so fools repeat their folly."

But thanks be to God, I could not get there—I could not access it! All I reached was that new angel-designed man cave of great joy. Instead of wallowing, I found myself laughing . . . in great excitement. In the midst of my pain, I rejoiced because I had truly been set free from the dreaded "Black Dog" depression. Even in my frenzy, the Lord proved that He had set this captive free.

In transparency, I confess a part of me was a bit sad. I just wanted to have a pity party for an extended time, but the door had been permanently closed. I had been healed. To this very day I have not been able to access that dreadful place, no matter how dire my circumstances. And I certainly have dipped into emotional black ops from time to time, especially as I battled the swine flu and its aftermath. But I've never returned to that trash pit of hell where I used to take refuge during painful times.

As I have already written, the causes of depression may be as varied as the number of people who have been so afflicted. In healing ministry, however, we can unpack the specific causes with supplicants, so that their impact is rendered null and void. I queried earlier whether depression is a learned behavior, but why does it matter? Through prayer any behavior can be unlearned. Sometimes depression can be triggered by a biochemical "abnormality" or, perhaps, rooted in our DNA. Women sometimes experience physical and emotional postpartum depression following giving birth. Grief—due to loss of jobs, deaths, relationships, moves, and so on—is also on the long list of suspect causes. The good news is, however, that our God is greater!

When we pray for people suffering from depression, we must also pray into the chemistry of their brains. We can battle depression with prayer, and when necessary (with the recommendation of an attending physician) we use prescription drugs. Even secular talk therapy and psychotherapy can sometimes bring relief to the afflicted. But, without exception, particularly in those who know Jesus Christ as their Lord and Savior, never leave Him out of the treatment plan. Jesus is the only treatment option without potential adverse effects.

Today, because of our ability to access most medical information on the internet, I would be remiss to not caution against self-diagnosis. If depression is suspected, then we should seek to be evaluated by a professional to either confirm our suspicion with a formal diagnosis or help discover what else may be troubling us.

Should you or someone you know be professionally diagnosed with clinical depression and are currently on medication, it is vital that the medication be continued until the treating physician determines it is safe to stop. Sometimes people begin to feel better and just stop taking their meds. Some patients prevail upon their physicians to allow them to stop prematurely. It is important to know that stopping treatment when medications eventually begin working may cause more harm than never having taken them. Be patient with yourself and with your medical providers. Your goal must be to sustain your healing after you stop your medications—with, and only with, your doctor's supervision.

Christians often undermine healing that is evidenced through the work of treating physicians and medications. Some think that if healing is not spontaneous and miraculous, that it is not God's doing at all. But they are unequivocally wrong! God inspired men and women to discover medications and treatments that would help His people. He inspired men and women to become medical practitioners, even men and women who may not yet know Him. There is nothing less miraculous about healing simply because it results from taking medication.

Are some of your supplicants defiant toward their doctors? If so, they may also be defiant toward God. I am not saying that physicians are infallible—they make mistakes, no argument there. However, if the attitude toward doctors is defiant (perhaps because physicians seemingly have authority over their patients), then I suspect something may be blocking the relationship with God Himself, not just the doc. Supplicants should ask the Lord to sift them and determine what, if anything, needs to change for them to be able to receive healing.

I hope you have noticed that not once have I referred to depression or any other disease as "my" depression or "my" illness. If you missed this nuance, please recognize it now. Whatever afflicts you is not yours. Illness is not from Jesus—it is from the enemy of our souls. Don't ever claim illness as your possession. Don't own it.

That said, unfortunately it is not uncommon to encounter supplicants—even when they are believers in Christ—who not only own their illness but also enthusiastically embrace it. In some instances, people identify so closely with their illness that it becomes a faithful companion. Some folks may have been afflicted with illness for so long that they are comfortable with it. They may even become so intimate with their disease that it has become their identity.

Healing ministers should discern if a supplicant is so disposed, because it may render them resistant to healing. Though sick people don't enjoy their illness, they may become enamored with the unusual amount of attention they now receive from family and friends because of it. If you suspect a supplicant may be clinging to such identities as "depressant," "brain injured," or "cancer patient," ask Jesus to gently reveal whether he or she is fearful that the kindness and affection they are receiving might evaporate if they became well. If Jesus shows you this, then please suggest the person seek inner healing from an experienced prayer minister so that they can heal that fear and receive their healing.

If you have a supplicant who is struggling with depression, please have them read John 14:27, which Jesus spoke to His downhearted disciples, several times: "Peace I leave with you; my peace I give you. I do not give to you as the world gives. Do not let your hearts be troubled and do not be afraid." Then have them read it several more times. Let Jesus' words truly sink in.

Then ask them to lift their eyes heavenward as they read and absorb the brilliant words of Psalm 121:

> I lift up my eyes to the mountains—
> where does my help come from?
> My help comes from the LORD,
> the Maker of heaven and earth.
> He will not let your foot slip—

he who watches over you will not slumber;

indeed, he who watches over Israel

will neither slumber nor sleep.

The LORD watches over you—

the LORD is your shade at your right hand;

the sun will not harm you by day,

nor the moon by night.

The LORD will keep you from all harm—

he will watch over your life;

the LORD will watch over your coming and going

both now and forevermore.

Beloved, our Lord Jesus Christ will never leave people nor forsake them. He is their Maker and is with them always. He will watch over their lives.

Sir Winston Churchill said, "If you are going through Hell, keep going . . ."

So may it be with our supplicants who struggle with depression. Help them to press on in the face of aridity and disenchantment . . . press on! Give it all to the Lord; lay it all at the foot of His cross. Pray for His rewiring of their brains. Pray, in the name of the one and only Jesus Christ, that depression leaves them. Pray that their minds and emotions are recovered in the perfection in which they were created.

UNWORTHINESS AND LOW SELF-ESTEEM

I'll call nobodies and make them somebodies;
I'll call the unloved and make them beloved.
In the place where they yelled out, "You're nobody!"
they're calling you "God's living children."
—ROMANS 9:25 THE MESSAGE

I once ministered to a woman in her mid-sixties who had a traumatic memory of her high school prom night. It had haunted her for forty-eight years! She recalled her father shaking the hand of her prom date as her date deposited her at her home. She noticed that her father had a wad of money in his hand that he slipped into her date's palm. She had no idea, until that very moment, that her father had paid this young man to take her to her prom. We had a lot of work to do on that memory! Her self-esteem had been demolished since high school. Forty-eight years later the raw emotions of that night still traumatized her.

Of course, this precious woman was justified in the emotional pain she felt that night about her unworthiness and the anger she directed at her father. But because her feelings were never dealt with, and memories real or imagined have enormous power over our lives, there had been no benefit gained from the experience. She left home as soon after her graduation as possible. She had regularly nurtured and refreshed this memory whenever it came to mind. It had festered and grown into an emotional boil that needed lancing. Through prayer and inner healing, we reframed her recollection of that night, with Jesus present. She watched the Lord set her free from this trauma as she embraced Jesus' unfathomable love for her. She commented to me that Jesus "had hung naked for me on the cross and took my lifelong shame to the grave with Him."

Her healing included a willingness to accept the truth of our triune God that had been tainted by her corrupted view of her earthly father. She was joyously grateful for her new and clear vision of God's grace and love. She let me know that she had come to realize her feelings of unworthiness had been rooted in a deep self-hatred that she had carried all those years.

An individual's self-esteem reflects their subjective evaluation of their overall personal worth. It is not unusual for the view of our worthiness to be damaged at an early age, the result being an incredibly distorted image within us. When we finally come to recognize that we have been duped into believing the worst about ourselves, we can begin to believe that it is never too late for our loving God to set us free. By inviting Jesus Christ to be present in our memories (see chapter 18, "Painful Memories"), we can reframe those painful memories and allow Him to help us discover His truth in the midst of them. Often, also, if we had a tyrant for an earthly father, or no father at all, our image of God could be distorted and needs to be confronted and healed in accordance with the truth about who He is and how much He loves us.

To add salt to the wounds of those who have been self-condemned by their low self-esteem, we know that unworthiness is one of the top ten road blocks to receiving healing in this area. Double jeopardy! Not only do we feel unworthy, but our sense of unworthiness *also* prohibits us from being healed.

Healing ministers must be on high alert whenever we encounter low self-esteem, self-loathing, and self-condemnation in our supplicants. We will need to immediately begin ministering to their distorted image of who God is and how He sees them. If they only knew and accepted the reality and truth of God's unfathomable love and His delight in them, they wouldn't waste another day lamenting and wallowing in a lie.

Are you worthy? Of course you are not! Not by, or of, your own merit, that is. I know I am certainly not. No one on this earth is worthy, except those who have received God's offer of salvation and redemption through faith in the power and authority of the Lord Jesus Christ. Those who believe in the person of God's Son, Jesus Christ, are loved beyond measure; they are squeaky-clean forgiven and have been made worthy by the supreme sacrifice of His own blood. Let's look at some of the verses attesting to this in the Bible:

All this is evidence that God's judgment is right, and as a result you will be counted worthy of the kingdom of God. (2 Thessalonians 1:5)

Isaiah maintained this same emphasis:

If each grain of sand on the seashore were numbered
and the sum labeled "chosen of God,"
They'd be numbers still, not names;
salvation comes by personal selection.
God doesn't count us; he calls us by name.
Arithmetic is not his focus. (Romans 9:20–27 THE MESSAGE)

C. S. Lewis said, "Christ died for men precisely because men are not worth dying for; to make them worth it."[1]

Lead musician and vocalist Michael Grayson and his former band Mikeschair wrote and recorded a song inspired by Lewis's quote. That song, "Someone Worth Dying For," debuted on their final CD that was released, *A Beautiful Life*. You can find the video on YouTube, recorded in 2011. God bless this talented young man! If you got through watching and listening to this music video of "Someone Worth Dying For" without shedding a tear, then I urge you to listen again, and this time, open your heart to allow the Lover of your precious soul to convince you that you really were worthy of dying for! If you had been the only person on the earth when Jesus came to establish the new covenant, He would still have come—for you alone. Here are a few more Scripture verses that remind us of that.

> God has united you with Christ Jesus. . . . Christ made us right with God; he made us pure and holy, and he freed us from sin. (1 Corinthians 1:30 NLT)

> But that's no life for you. You learned Christ! . . . Since, then, . . . everything—and I do mean everything—connected with that old way of life has to go. It's rotten through and through. Get rid of it! And then take on an entirely new way of life—a God-fashioned life, a life renewed from the inside and working itself into your conduct as God accurately reproduces his character in you. (Ephesians 4:20–24 The Message)

> But you are the ones chosen by God . . . to be . . . God's instruments . . . to tell others of the night-and-day difference he made for you—from nothing to something, from rejected to accepted. (1 Peter 2:9–10 The Message)

Healing ministers, if supplicants reject His provision for them and still listen to a lying, mocking tongue—"Nah, God's love, acceptance, and redemption are not for the likes of me"—then you and your prayer partner need to redouble your prayers for the supplicants to become "ripe" for healing. Either they don't know or won't accept that Jesus has died for them already. Either way, only prayer can soften their resolve. During this time in between resistance and healing, it is imperative that supplicants feel listened to, loved, and lifted on the stretchers of your prayers for healing in their bodies, minds, and spirits. Your steadfastness as a healing minister will be strengthened as you focus on the truth of who Jesus is and His authority to do whatever is necessary to retrieve His lost lambs. Let these scriptures minister to you as you minister to others:

> Jesus told this simple story, but they had no idea what he was talking about. So he tried agian. "I'll be explicit, then. I am the Gate for the sheep. All those others are up to no good—sheep stealers, every one of them. But the sheep didn't listen to them. I am the Gate. Anyone who goes through me will be cared for—will freely go in and out, and find pasture. A thief is only there to steal and kill and destroy. I came so they can have real and eternal life, more and better life than they ever dreamed of." (John 10:6–10 The Message)

> If you believe, you will receive whatever you ask for in prayer. (Matthew 21:22)

> For everyone who asks receives; the one who seeks finds; and to the one who knocks, the door will be opened. (Matthew 7:8)

As straightforward as Matthew 7:8 appears, I found *The Message* translation of Matthew 7:7–11 especially insightful:

> Don't bargain with God. Be direct. Ask for what you need. This isn't a cat-and-mouse, hide-and-seek game we're in. If your child asks for bread, do you trick him with sawdust? If he asks for fish,

do you scare him with a live snake on his plate? As bad as you are, you wouldn't think of such a thing . . . don't you think the God who conceived you in love will be even better?

On any Sunday morning, in any Anglican church, before the congregation is invited to come to the Lord's Table to receive the Eucharist, or the Holy Communion—a sacrament to affirm our binding covenant with our triune God—we should pray the Prayer of Humble Access, written by Archbishop Cranmer of Canterbury in 1548:

> We do not presume to come to this thy Table, O merciful Lord, trusting in our own righteousness, but in thy manifold and great mercies. We are not worthy so much as to gather up the crumbs under thy Table. But thou art the same Lord, whose property is always to have mercy: Grant us therefore, gracious Lord, so to eat the flesh of thy dear Son Jesus Christ, and to drink his blood, that our sinful bodies may be made clean by his body, and our souls washed through his most precious blood, and that we may evermore dwell in him, and he in us. Amen.

As we begin to derive our identity and worth from Jesus, as our Lord and Savior, we can confess that we are not worthy so much as to gather up the crumbs under His table. We gladly confess this state of affairs without subscribing to it—for we know that it is but a half-truth, isn't it? We are certainly not worthy in and of ourselves, but we know that our belief and confident faith in Jesus Christ has made us worthy. Might you now join the millions of others, including me, who recite this prayer without feeling condemnation? Let's put a stake through the very heart of any lie that attempts to deceive us in the future. If you are in Christ, you have been made worthy!

When those called to healing prayer ministry have grasped this truth, their prayers for healing will transform the lives of those for whom they pray. Recall the Roman centurion who told Jesus in Matthew 8:8 (NLT): "Lord, I am not worthy to have you come into my home. Just say the word from where you are, and my servant will be healed." In stating that he was not worthy, it is exactly like us praying the Prayer of Humble Access. We can state the obvious fact that we are not worthy, without compromising the truth that, in Christ, we are worthy! The centurion's servant was healed instantly because Jesus delighted in the faith the soldier demonstrated in coming to Him and asking for healing.

I am passionate on this topic because I, too, was a captive who believed I lacked worth. I recall my math teacher at Plymouth College Prep School in the UK, who condemned me publicly as a seven-year-old: "Mumford, you are useless and will amount to nothing." Just now, for a split second, I palpably felt the pain of those words searing my soul as if it happened today. Though at the time I believed every word that cursed me, by the grace of God, I was eventually delivered from this condemnation. In actuality it had been true, then, as I was at the bottom of every class except geography and music. But after learning that Sir Winston Churchill, also at the age of seven, had been told the very same thing, I saw how ridiculous it was to cling to the words of that reckless teacher from my past. When I learned about Churchill, it was as though the off switch in my brain had been suddenly flipped on! I was sent to a new school where I achieved a "first" in science. Jesus had set me free from all self-condemnation, and I was rendered a new man!

This is your life; it's not a dress rehearsal. It is worth repeating, again and again, to ourselves: "Don't let our past ruin our present or our future!" Amen? If this is your struggle, as it was mine, I pray that Jesus will redirect you into the "new you" that He will reveal as you accept His love. Let's take a fresh look at Jesus and give ourselves permission to believe that Jesus wants us to live our lives in His abundance. Nothing less!

I hate to keep repeating myself, but frankly, we cannot read or hear this enough. In Mark 12:31, Jesus said: "The second [commandment] is this: 'Love your neighbor as yourself.' There is no commandment greater than these." Let this verse sink in . . . "love your neighbor as yourself." If you do not feel worthy and are afflicted with self-loathing and low self-esteem—you are not obeying God! You see, if you will not accept the love that God has for you, embracing and loving yourself, then you are incapable of loving your neighbor, no matter how much you profess to prefer your neighbor to yourself. Contempt begets contempt. Love begets love. "We love because he first loved us" (1 John 4:19). If you can't receive His love, then just what do you think you could possibly offer your neighbor? I know this may be painful to hear, but to not tell you would be dreadfully more agonizing in the end!

A fellow healing minister figured out that she needed to tell supplicants that it "was okay to love yourselves!" She tells all who have long held themselves in contempt that it's even okay to form a sort of crush on themselves as they discover how unique and glorious they are. No, not the self-centered, hyper-introspective adoration that narcissists may have for themselves; but the grounded and obedient love for self that the children of God possess—borne out of their personal love relationships with Jesus Christ.

Beloved, both you and your supplicants need to hear continuously that you are fearfully and wonderfully made. Say to yourself and to them: "When God called you by your name from your mother's womb, He took you into His loving arms, inspected every square inch of you, and rejoiced over what He saw. Hand-designed by His committee of Three: the Father, the Son, and the Holy Spirit—at the very moment of your debut on earth, there was a raucous celebration in the heavens! Not one regret does He have in you, His created one. Won't you please yield to His irresistible love for you? Please let Him show you how He sees you! What's not to love?"

What does the opposite of unworthiness look like? Ah well . . . gentleness, boldness, fearlessness, unashamed, healthy boundaries, self-acceptance, not envious, nonjudgmental, delighting in others, magnanimous, inclusive, self-confident, joyful, buoyant, loving, gracious, merciful, and compassionate. Hear this: "If God is for us, who can be against us?" (Romans 8:31). The opposite of unworthiness is to be joined to Jesus Christ and to fully know that "The one who calls you is faithful, and he will do it" (1 Thessalonians 5:24).

Before preaching or speaking at healing conferences, churches, seminaries, or even the Pentagon, I am in the habit of reading from the words of Paul found in 1 Corinthians 2:1–5. These words have helped me so many times and have given me a boost of confidence to be able to present the healing gospel of Jesus Christ:

> And so it was with me, brothers and sisters. When I came to you, I did not come with eloquence or human wisdom as I proclaimed to you the testimony about God. For I resolved to know nothing while I was with you except Jesus Christ and him crucified. I came to you in weakness with great fear and trembling. My message and my preaching were not with wise and persuasive words, but with a demonstration of the Spirit's power, so that your faith might not rest on human wisdom, but on God's power.

Paul, credited with first evangelizing the Gentiles, understood that it was God's power—not his or anyone else's—that could impact the people he was sent to. Just say the word of Jesus . . . using only His words, revealing only His truth, with only His spirit indwelling us.

The love of God is not measured by worth. With God we do not need to prove ourselves in any way. The Lord loves us without limits. We were made worthy through His cross. Jesus lived and died for us to have abundant life. May you truly receive His gift. If you are a healing minister who has received this gift, you are to be His vessel, in praying and ministering to others so that they will know their worth.

Rejoice in the words found in Psalm 103:6–18 (THE MESSAGE):

> GOD makes everything come out right; he puts victims back on their feet. . . . GOD is sheer mercy and grace; not easily angered, he's rich

in love. He doesn't endlessly nag and scold, nor hold grudges forever. He doesn't treat us as our sins deserve, nor pay us back in full for our wrongs. As high as heaven is over the earth, so strong is his love to those who fear him. And as far as sunrise is from sunset, he has separated us from our sins. . . . He knows us inside and out, keeps in mind that we're made of mud. Men and women don't live very long; like wildflowers they spring up and blossom, But a storm snuffs them out just as quickly, leaving nothing to show they were here. God's love, though, is ever and always, eternally present to all who fear him, making everything right for them and their children as they follow his Covenant ways and remember to do whatever he said.

Prayer to Set a Captive Free

Lord God, I am a captive of my past. Somewhere in my life I came to believe that I am unworthy. My heart and my mind have accepted this lie. Your Word says that You came to set captives like me free. Jesus, please separate me from the past and help me to truly know You as Lord and Savior. I want to live my life in boldness with You by my side. Just say the word, Lord, and I will be released from this prison cell of insecurity, self-condemnation, self-loathing, and unworthiness. I rebuke any lies that have hindered my life and, now, shake the chains free from my neck, wrists, and ankles. Please guide me, protect me, love me, and help me grow into who You called me to be. Allow me to see myself as You do and to receive Your love. Out of Your unfathomable love, day by day, help me grow to love myself as You do and demonstrate that love to my neighbors in Your precious name. Thank You, dear Lord—Father, Son, and Holy Spirit—for making me in Your image and freeing me, this day, to live my life in Your fullness! Amen.

15

GUILT AND SHAME

The one who sins is the one who will die. The
child will not share the guilt of the parent,
nor will the parent share the guilt of the
child. The righteousness of the righteous will
be credited to them, and the wickedness of
the wicked will be charged against them.
—EZEKIEL 18:20

Many people for whom I pray are haunted by lingering memories that cling like Velcro to their souls. A later chapter on memories and inner healing will more thoroughly address this issue, but it is prudent for us to consider the power they have in our lives to create guilt and shame.

Sometimes guilt is a learned behavior. I've noticed that most people who are religious, but not necessarily intimate with God, manifest more than the usual amount of guilt. The threat of hell or Sheol holds a lot of sway for folks who painstakingly follow the rules (the tenets and laws of the faith basis to which they belong). Their default emotion is guilt. If they are the head of the church picnic and it rains the day of, somehow they feel responsible! Their self-condemnation is over-the-top and breaks my heart. Jesus did not die for us to wallow in guilt and shame, especially when He would likely disagree that you had any grounds for it. The world is a tough enough place without becoming your own judge and executioner.

Given that unforgiveness is one of the strongest blocks to receiving healing, it's clear that if we won't forgive ourselves and choose to continue to hold on to guilt and shame, it will block our healing. My experiences have led me to understand that the minutia—those small, often trivial details stemming out of our guilt and shame—must be pushed out of the way to get to healing. I'd even go as far as saying that guilt and shame can, themselves, be a block to healing. Often borne out of guilt and shame is a sense of unworthiness. If you don't believe or feel worthy to receive God's gifts, you surely will not be healed! Your internal narrative may be something like, "Lord, I am so ashamed and guilty of events in my past, that You cannot possibly love me. Why then would You see me as worthy to heal?" Not true, dear friend! That is not an accurate understanding of God.

Like a boil that needs to be lanced, so must these issues be cleansed and eliminated. By allowing His light—the light of truth to illumine all dark spaces in our innermost beings—we can both heal *and* provide for the well-being of all who love us! Can you see how the power of shame and guilt are working against healing in a person's life? Is it time for them to confess? May I suggest that you consider asking them to write a confession on paper and then, with Jesus present, burning that paper? Haven't these issues constricted their life long enough? What might they be carrying that our Jesus wants to unload and have given to Him, so they can be set free?

What is guilt? Merriam-Webster defines *guilt*, in addition to being the finding by a jury or judge, as:

13. 2 a. the state of one who has committed an offense especially consciously; 2 b. feelings of deserving blame

especially for imagined offenses or from a sense of inade-
quacy: self-reproach;

14. a feeling of deserving blame for offenses

PsychologyToday.com states:

The negative emotion of guilt can be paralyzing for some people. A
person can feel guilty for something he did, for something he didn't
do, for something he thought he did, or for not doing enough for
another person. Certainly, if a person causes harm to another, then
guilt and remorse are natural. This feeling can catalyze a person to
apologize, correct the wrong, and do better in the future. These are
appropriate reactions.[1]

Consider the last sentence of the above quotation—"These are
appropriate reactions." Not to contradict what I wrote earlier, but it is
important to note that there is such a thing as healthy guilt. Healthy
guilt often arises at or out of moments in which we are tempted to act
in a sinful manner. It often stops us cold from things such as shoplift-
ing, running red lights, lying, cheating, and so forth. Paul described
something similar to healthy guilt in 2 Corinthians 7:9–10 (NLT):

Now I am glad . . . not because it hurt you, but because the pain
caused you to repent and change your ways. It was the kind of sorrow
God wants his people to have, so you were not harmed . . . in any way.
For the kind of sorrow God wants us to experience leads us away from
sin and results in salvation. There's no regret for that kind of sorrow.
But worldly sorrow, which lacks repentance, results in spiritual death.

Paul was saying, in the above passage, that the kind of sorrow (or
guilt) that comes from God results in our safety and freedom, whereas
worldly sorrow results in spiritual death . . . experienced as a haunting,

unrelenting sense of guilt. In differentiating between worldly sorrow (or guilt) and God's "gift" of sorrow, Paul allowed for what I call "healthy guilt."

In 2002, author Philip Yancey wrote an article for *Christianity Today* entitled "Guilt Good and Bad." In it he wrote, "A sense of guilt, vastly underappreciated, deserves our gratitude, for only such a powerful force can nudge us toward repentance and reconciliation with those we have harmed."[2]

Yancey went on to write, "Martin Luther, in his early days as a monk, would daily wear out his confessors with as many as six straight hours of introspection about minuscule sins and unhealthy thoughts. 'My son, God is not angry with you: it is you, who are angry with God,' said one of his exasperated advisers. Luther eventually came to agree that his fear of sinning actually showed a lack of faith, both in his ability to live purely in an impure world, and in Christ's provision for his sin. 'To diagnose smallpox you do not have to probe each pustule, nor do you heal each separately,' he concluded."[3]

Finally, in part quoting David Wolpe, acclaimed as the most influential Jew in America, an article in *USA Today* says: "Facing up to the hurt we cause others with cruel speech or callous acts, and to our myriad failures to meet the marks God sets for living a true and good life, 'makes forgiveness meaningful, not merely a catchphrase.'"[4]

One thing is for sure: no one is advocating that we should carry around burdensome buckets of guilt throughout our lives. Not even "healthy" guilt should be internalized only to become the source of our emotional and spiritual hauntings. So, what do we do with our guilt? Though this is common practice in my faith tradition, I recognize it may not be in yours. In any event, knowing the fruit that is harvested as a result, I commend to you confession. Confession combined with the Reconciliation of the Penitent (a liturgy found in the *Book of Common Prayer*) would take care of us very nicely.

Even if I tried, I couldn't say this any better than how it is stated in Psalm 32:1–5 (NLT). These are God's instructions on how we are to deal with our guilt:

> Oh, what joy for those whose disobedience is forgiven, whose sin
>   is put out of sight!
> Yes, what joy for those whose record the LORD has cleared of
>   guilt,
> whose lives are lived in complete honesty!
> When I refused to confess my sin, my body wasted away, and I
>   groaned all day long.
> Day and night your hand of discipline was heavy on me.
> My strength evaporated like water in the summer heat.
> Finally, I confessed all my sins to you and stopped trying to hide
>   my guilt.
> I said to myself, "I will confess my rebellion to the LORD."
> And you forgave me! All my guilt is gone.

Since we've already established that guilt and shame frequently accompany one another, we need to understand that they are not the same; they are uniquely different from one another.

Psychology Today says: "Shame is guilt's close handmaiden. They are two closely related emotions, though guilt concerns others, and shame is more internal. A person may not have done anything particular, but shame bubbles up within. And a person may feel internally ashamed about themselves, yet does not feel any guilt toward others whatsoever."[5]

In a post titled "Shame: A Concealed, Contagious, and Dangerous Emotion," Mary C. Lamia, PhD, further sets shame apart from guilt:

> Shame is often confused with guilt—an emotion we might experience
> as a result of a wrongdoing about which we might feel remorseful and
> wish to make amends. Where we will likely have an urge to admit

guilt, or talk with others about a situation that left us with guilty feelings, it is much less likely that we will broadcast our shame. In fact, we'll most likely conceal what we feel because shame does not make a distinction between an action and the self. Therefore, with shame, "bad" behavior is not separate from a "bad" self as it is with guilt.[6]

What is shame? The Oxford Dictionary defines it as "a painful feeling of humiliation or distress caused by the consciousness of wrong or foolish behavior."

In her article cited above, Dr. Lamia further elaborated on the elements of shame:

> Shame informs us of an internal state of inadequacy, unworthiness, dishonor, regret, or disconnection. Shame is a clear signal that our positive feelings have been interrupted. Another person or a circumstance can trigger shame in us, but so can a failure to meet our own ideals or standards. Given that shame can lead us to feel as though our whole self is flawed, bad, or subject to exclusion, it motivates us to hide or to do something to save face. So it is no wonder that shame avoidance can lead to withdrawal or to addictions that attempt to mask its impact.[7]

The late John Wimber, founder of Vineyard Church, once sat next to a man on an airplane. In the Spirit, Wimber saw a big letter *A* written across the man's forehead. Wimber simply asked the man how long it had been going on. The man knew immediately what he meant and expressed his guilt and shame. He asked, "How did you know?" Wimber explained that it had been written on his face! In the words of Psalm 44:15: "I live in disgrace all day long, and my face is covered with shame." Like the large, red *A* that Hester Prynne was forced to wear in Nathaniel Hawthorne's novel *The Scarlet Letter*, the *A* Wimber saw written on the man's forehead he discerned stood for adultery and recognized the visible shame on the man's face. The rest of the story is that the man confessed and Wimber introduced him to Jesus, who set him free to go and sin no more.

Helping someone be set free from guilt and shame requires allowing them to confess sinful behavior(s) as they unpack their story in a safe, nonjudgmental setting where Jesus Christ can meet their felt needs. Sometimes, however, guilt and shame can take up residence in a supplicant, despite the supplicant's innocence or lack of wrongdoing. Even if a supplicant is not guilty, shame can be internalized. That's why confession is so good for us. Neither the prayer minister nor the supplicant need sort out whether one's shame is deserved, because in the process of confession it will all be clarified. When we humbly and voluntarily confess our sins to a prayer minister or clergyperson, the absolution that follows, in Jesus Christ's name, is enough to set former captives absolutely free!

Would you take a moment to imagine that God does not want your supplicants to be plagued by shame and guilt? Can you even grasp that feeling? What would it actually feel like for them to be totally set free from such a burden? What skeletons are hiding in their closets? God does not want them walking around with this cloud of shame and guilt. May the joy of the Lord become their strength.

Perhaps you yourself need to be set free from guilt and shame. God sent His Son, Jesus Christ, to set the captives free. Before studying the healing of memories, you can begin to experience some freedom simply believing that the accuser in your spirit is not God! The accuser is, and has always been, the evil one or our own self-condemnation. Recall what Dr. Lambia wrote earlier: "Another person or a circumstance can trigger shame in us, but so can a failure to meet our own ideals or standards."

Aha! There you have it. Shame can be triggered when *we* fail to meet our own ideals or standards. Don't even think about laying that on God. He is not your accuser! Too often, we do that job to ourselves without the evil one even insinuating himself into our messes!

So exactly who is your accuser? If not God, then who? If not God, then whom does that accuser think they are? If not God, my friend, then how dare they (or you, yourself) accuse you?

Guilt is mentioned 189 times in the New International Version translation of the Bible, and *shame* is cited 147 times. And yet, regardless of how often these two troublesome words are referenced, if you believe Jesus and love Him, you will know that Jesus has your back. Read this quote from Romans 8:1 (NLT): "So now there is no condemnation for those who belong to Christ Jesus." This is a prescription verse I hand out daily to many supplicants.

How about we read that again one more time? Perhaps you, like me, would benefit from even writing that verse and posting it onto your bathroom mirrors so that the first thing you see when you get out of bed in the morning is this verse reminding you that God is not your accuser. Indeed, the one who knows you best and loves you most is your greatest advocate in this life!

With that hopefully cleared up for you, let's consider another type of guilt . . .

Survivor's Guilt

I bump into evidence of survivor's guilt in many people and, most especially, in combat veterans. It is not unusual when a soldier is relieved by another for patrol duty and subsequently learns that something devastating happened during that patrol that the survivor instantly feels guilty for having stayed behind. Survivor's guilt wreaks havoc not only in those materially impacted but also in those who are in relationship with survivors.

The internal narrative of a survivor can quickly become repetitive self-indictment: "It should have been me. If only it had been me. If only I would have gone on that patrol instead . . ."

Let's take a look at this from a different perspective—one that is most likely shared by the deceased *and* our God. How do they view the situation? I believe that they'd want the survivor to live life to the fullest. The deceased would likely encourage the survivor to live fully and embrace the life still before him. And our Lord would remind us that it wasn't our time to depart this life, that He has more for us to do.

Quite frankly, survivor's guilt is, though seldom acknowledged as such, collateral damage. It robs life from the living as if they were dead. Make the most of life in honor of and out of deference to the life or lives that were snuffed out. The enemy declares victory when God's children pile guilt and shame upon themselves. Let go of it, friends.

I do realize, of course, that combat is only one arena in which survivor's guilt attaches itself to those who remain among the living. I know supplicants who, while being treated for one disease or another and making strides on their personal healing journey, must reckon with family, friends, or coworkers who have lost their battles with illnesses or have died by accidental death. Sweet Amanda from Florida, while clinging to Jesus' healing gifts, ultimately outlived her dire fatal medical prognosis by eight years. Her experimental treatments were excruciatingly painful, but she never complained until she contracted shingles. When she sheepishly asked for healing prayer, she prefaced her request by admitting she felt dreadfully guilty for complaining while so many of her fellow cancer patients were losing their battles. Amanda dismissed her bout with shingles as petty considering her deceased and dying friends. "How dare I whine about shingles when I've been spared while so many others have died!"

Even survivor's guilt, despite being predicated upon actual events, is false guilt. If we suffer it, we believe a lie and bare false witness against ourselves! False guilt is self-abuse. It puts an unbearable burden upon us, one that we were never intended to shoulder. It is sinful, and we must stop now.

Worldly guilt (or sorrow) is a feeling that results when you tell yourself (truthfully or not) that you did something wrong. Healthy guilt is a feeling that occurs when you have actually done something wrong—such as deliberately harming another. In the case of survivor's guilt, events are entirely out of your control; you have done nothing wrong. Worldly guilt is not from God. As Paul warned us in 2 Corinthians 8, it is unhealthy and will kill you. I know the Lord wants neither your life nor your usefulness to Him impeded by carrying a cross He never asked you to bear.

Charles Spurgeon, author and British Reformed Baptist preacher, recognized how gruesome and debilitating false guilt is to a person's spiritual growth, diminishing a person's ability to receive Christ's love due to such self-abuse. Spurgeon told his students, "Learn how to say no, it will do you more good than learning Latin. Say no to these false accusations."

It's vitally important to help your supplicants unpack their bulging suitcases of shame and guilt and surrender them to their Savior, Jesus Christ. You know they are tired of carrying that heavy weight with them wherever they go. Scripture tells us that we should seek first the kingdom of God and all God's provision will be added to us. Encourage your supplicants to take the next twenty-one days and lift their faces to God every time they are haunted by the memory of something that causes them shame and guilt. Then encourage them to say out loud, "Thank You, God, for reminding me to ask Your forgiveness and to surrender this memory to You. I freely do that now and ask You to separate me from my sins and my feelings of guilt and shame. Thank You for loving me and sacrificing Yourself for me."

Here is the good news of Hebrews 10:1–3, 7, 10 (NLT):

The old system under the law of Moses was only a shadow, a dim preview of the good things to come. . . . The sacrifices under that system were repeated again and again, year after year, but they were never able to provide perfect cleansing for those who came to worship. If they could have provided perfect cleansing, the sacrifices would have stopped, for the worshipers would have been purified once for all time, and their feelings of guilt would have disappeared. But instead, those sacrifices actually reminded them of their sins year after year. . . . Then I [Jesus] said, "Look, I have come to do your will, O God—as is written about me in the Scriptures. . . ." For God's will was for us to be made holy by the sacrifice of the body of Jesus Christ, once for all time.

Before God executed His great plan for our redemption, He provided for annual animal sacrifices to be made to help us feel forgiven. But the blood of sheep and goats could not expunge our internal narratives of guilt, much less our shame! By His grace, He provided for those rites to help us—and yet, for the most part, this annual ritual only made us remember how very guilty we were. Until Jesus was born and began His ministry, we remained guilty and ashamed even though we understood that God really did love us. But when God finally sent Jesus to earth, He ordained that only by the sacrifice of Jesus' body could we be forgiven.

And it would be just once, one sacrifice, for all time!

And since we have a great High Priest [Jesus] who rules over God's house, let us go right into the presence of God with sincere hearts fully trusting him. For our guilty consciences have been sprinkled with Christ's blood to make us clean, and our bodies have been washed with pure water. (Hebrews 10:21–22 NLT)

I want to end this chapter on guilt and shame on this note: the former Archbishop of Canterbury of the Church of England, Rowan Williams, wrote the following words that I find very inspirational and healing. Consider how people were drawn to Christ's love and joy as they were set free from their shame and guilt!

When reading the Gospels, you sometimes get the impression that if anywhere in ancient Galilee you heard a loud noise and a lot of laughter and singing, you could be reasonably sure that Jesus of Nazareth was around somewhere nearby.[8]

Be set free, dear friends, from your guilt and shame, and help your supplicant do the same, for your deliverer has come, and He awaits the acceptance of His invitation to let go of it all so that all of you will live your lives in abundance.

16

UNFORGIVENESS

[Forgive], just as in Christ God forgave you.
—EPHESIANS 4:32

Three decades of working within the healing ministry has taught me that unforgiveness is unequivocally the leading block to healing. I have come to look at unforgiveness as an emotional cancer, rotting away at the very soul of the person seeking healing. Oftentimes unforgiveness is not recognizable to supplicants themselves. In other instances, it is dismissed by supplicants and swept under the proverbial rug. But whether hidden or dismissed, it is constantly ready and willing to rear its ugly head and diminish the life of a supplicant who clings to it.

Unforgiveness is an open, gaping wound—both infected and infectious—that desperately requires the direct attention of healing ministers. It is the nemesis of healing. In Greek mythology, Nemesis was the goddess of punishment or vengeance. Ironically, the one who is most punished by unforgiveness is most definitely not the one who perpetrated the pain and wound. Rather, the one most cruelly punished is the one who will not forgive his or her perpetrator(s).

A friend and fellow healing minister was inspired to write extensively on this topic after the August 2004 interview of comic Joan Rivers by ABC's *20/20*. While discussing her husband Edgar's 1987 suicide, Rivers shared her response to people who say she'll see Edgar in heaven: "Oh, no, I won't! I don't ever want to see him again . . . what he did to me—I don't want to go into eternity with him. I'm still too angry!"[1] Here is an excerpt from my friend's Forgiveness Series in a weekly devotional, *Parting Thoughts*:

> The unforgiveness and resentment that Joan Rivers nurtured every day of her life for 17+ years, is more harmful and painful to her than ever was Edgar's suicide. It is unforgiveness that robbed her joy and perpetuated her pain.
>
> Wounds that we suffer at the hand of another are very painful. They trouble us in many ways and very often lead to physical illness. In the healing ministry, we frequently encounter the effects of emotional wounds as cancer, heart disease, backaches, immune system disorders, or a host of other illnesses. . . .
>
> Years ago, I ministered to a college sophomore who had an aggressive cancer which had progressed to the point that her life was in grave peril. I asked her to think back to an event [of great stress or trauma] that could be contributing to her illness.
>
> Later, she was able to share that she'd been sexually abused by a friend of her family. Together, we invited Jesus to go back to that time to be present with her as she spoke her forgiveness, out loud, to the person who abused her. She then asked Jesus to forgive that person as well. The Lord also led her to forgive her family members who had unwittingly exposed her to the one who had violated her innocence. She forgave each family member individually, and then asked Jesus to forgive them also. Finally, and most importantly, she forgave herself and embraced Jesus Christ's forgiveness of her. Today she is cancer-free, annual scans attest to her healing. She was healed, not just in her body—but in her mind and spirit as well.
>
> Sometimes we are called to forgive others for the wounds they

have inflicted upon us. Just as often, however, we must forgive our-selves for thoughts, words and deeds that we have said or done and for which no one else is to blame but ourselves. Self-blame keeps us from the love of God as surely as nurturing bitterness toward others. But whether it is against oneself or another, the sword of unforgiveness is destructive. It will kill you, if not in your body, it will destroy your mind and spirit. Though Joan Rivers's words may sound particularly calloused and harsh, many of us feel exactly the same way about person(s) or situation(s) in our lives, whether or not we are *willing to admit or discuss it*.[2]

I never cease to be astonished at the absolute power of un-forgiveness as I uncover the multilayered, lifelong, compounded, and accumulative issues that have contributed to the compost heap within the unforgiving supplicants I regularly encounter. Their visible (or perhaps hidden just below the surface) dung heaps pulsate with anticipation of the next insult or affront that will trigger their original wound. In an outburst of "justifiable" anger, they then waste all over a new offender, damaging yet another significant relation-ship in their lives.

A woman told me, "For me, to have a grudge is a reason for liv-ing!" Another supplicant, a rather prickly gentleman I ministered to, volunteered, "I hate my neighbor as much as I hate myself." Whoa! Jesus said, "'Love the Lord your God with all your heart and with all your soul and with all your mind. This is the first and greatest commandment. And the second is like it: 'Love your neighbor as yourself'" (Matthew 22:37–39). Both individuals had a lot of work to do on the greatest commandment. This is not the first time in this book you've read that you can't love your neighbor until you love yourself as your Creator loves you! Hence, with unforgiveness roiling around in your soul, there is little chance you'll be able to open your clenched fists to receive God's love for you.

What really gets to me is the repeated narrative spoken internally by so many people. Their heartbreaking accounts of trauma are often shared with me in a fashion similar to the following:

> I really don't want to talk about this because I am so embarrassed, but when I was seven I was sexually abused by my neighbor. I just found out that he died last week. His abuse went on until I was twelve. I have no idea why my mother had no clue. If she did know, then why didn't she ever confront him in my defense? I have more anger toward my mum than the guy who did this! Why did this happen to me? Why? Why? I couldn't tell anyone what was happening back then lest our neighbor make good on his threat to kill my mum, my dad, even my cat—if I ever told. Though I am old now—sixty-three, the memory of those horrible years has ruined my entire life, my marriage, my career, and many friendships.

This narrative is all too familiar. Though each person has a unique story, regardless of what, when, where, or how, the narratives I hear are, frankly, analogous to screams of rage: "Why have I allowed this perpetrator to steal my joy, my life, my very existence?"

It breaks my heart as it becomes clear that supplicants who present themselves for healing are carrying around the baggage of unforgiveness. It's so sad because they are not yet aware of what the Lord has shown me—that unforgiveness gives their perpetrator(s) continued and unbridled power over them! When perpetrators are not forgiven, their victims must expend untold energy to hide their unhealed scars. Burdened with the heavy weight of unforgiveness, they become ruined physically, in their bodies; emotionally, in their relationships with others; and spiritually, in their image of God.

The power of unforgiveness leaches into every area of the victims' lives. The trauma they carry is akin to living monuments of historical events that forever remind them of their pain and shame. The following was told to me by someone who heard the Rev. Dr. Sherry Adams (ordained clergy and licensed psychologist) preach in 2004 at Good Samaritan Episcopal Church in Paoli, Pennsylvania:

> In her Sunday sermon, Rev. Adams likened ongoing unforgiveness to a landlord who let out a room in his home to a tenant who never paid rent. The tenant rarely left the house, ate all the food in the landlord's fridge and pantry, used all the electricity and hot water, slammed doors and played loud music at all hours. The landlord grew increasingly perverse as his resentment and bitterness mounted. Family and friends eventually found it impossible to relate to the now isolated and embittered landlord. On the rare occasions when the landlord ventured out, he raged at anyone he encountered who looked, sounded, or behaved like his free-loading tenant who had taken over his home!

You might think that this is an exaggeration, but having practiced the ministry of healing with people for several decades, I found this analogy spot on. Supplicants who carry around unforgiveness of those who have wounded them are equally consumed in their bodies, minds, and spirits as was the landlord of the deadbeat tenant.

Whenever I minister to captives seeking healing prayer for serious illnesses, relationship difficulties, or spiritual isolation, I am saddened by their lack of understanding of the root of their maladies. Regardless of how many years they have been thus, when these victims finally receive healing prayer, our God opens their eyes and sets them free. He throws off their chains and breaks off any residual bondage with their perpetrator(s). When they are set free, their perpetrator(s) are immediately stripped of their power and rendered impotent through Jesus' precision healing surgery. And it doesn't matter if perpetrator(s) are dead, alive, or serving jail time; inner healing and healing prayer set their victims free!

Human nature, however, is such that we may not really want to let go of our bitterness and shame. After all, as victims, we feel particularly justified, or perhaps entitled, in nurturing our resentment. Rather than seeking ways to heal, we tend to "own" our trauma wounds, even wearing them as a badge or membership card in the brother- and sisterhood of victims. Thankfully even supplicants, reticent to surrender their "victim" status, will receive deliverance when they seek the Lord's help. Is it time to move from victim to victor to victory?

With a healing minister present, or a trusted fellow believer, or entirely on their own, supplicants can ask Jesus to come and be present with them (as though He is with them, in time and space, in the memory of their wound). Once they feel Jesus present with them, they should allow themselves one final time to recall in detail the trauma they suffered at another's hands. They can ask Jesus to come between them and the perpetrator(s) and permit Him to hear, out loud, all their anger, rage, denial, fear, depression, disgust, and contempt that come to their minds and cross their lips in this scene. If curse words are among them, they let them come; the Lord is so much stronger than any feelings or words they will speak out in this place.

With Jesus present at their side, they might speak their forgiveness out loud to the perpetrator(s). Forgive him, or her, or them, for all the wounds they have just recounted. They may press into Jesus, lean against Him if they can feel Him there, and ask Him to forgive their offenders as well. Of course, for them to receive Christ's forgiveness, the offender must ultimately come to Him on their own; but the supplicants asking Him to forgive will forever release them from any stronghold the perpetrator(s) may have on them. When they and Jesus are done, they should be sure to ask Him to forgive them as well for holding on to their pain for too long, hurting themselves, believing lies about themselves, and not loving themselves as He loves them.

It is their time, beloved—beyond their time actually—to be set free from the power of any perpetrator within the memories of trauma that have festered, or been fanned into flame, over the intervening years. Their body, mind, and spirit had been taken captive.

Sometimes wounds are metaphoric low-flying black clouds that follow us everywhere and obstruct the truth of Jesus' appraisal of our lives. As you read Lamentations 3:44, allow it to provoke examination of your innermost self: "You have covered yourself with a cloud so that no prayer can get through." My heart aches as I contemplate how many of God's children are encumbered by an impenetrable cloud of shame and pain through which no prayer can penetrate. One of your tasks as a healing minister is to help them claim the promise of Romans 8:1–2: "Therefore, there is now no condemnation for those who are in Christ Jesus, because through Christ Jesus the law of the Spirit who gives life has set you free from the law of sin and death."

> It's your supplicant's time to be set free from the past.
> It's their time to ask Jesus to scatter their low-flying black
> clouds.
> It is their time to move from victim, to victor, to *victory*!

Know this, however, that if they have not yet forgiven the perpetrator(s) in their lives or asked Jesus to forgive them as well, they remain *their* prisoner. Consider what King David wrote:

> Some sat in darkness, in utter darkness,
> prisoners suffering in iron chains,
> because they rebelled against God's commands
> and despised the plans of the Most High.
> So he subjected them to bitter labor;
> they stumbled, and there was no one to help.
> Then they cried to the LORD in their trouble,
> and he saved them from their distress.
> He brought them out of darkness, the utter darkness,

and broke away their chains.
Let them give thanks to the LORD for his unfailing love
and his wonderful deeds for mankind,
for he breaks down gates of bronze
and cuts through bars of iron. (Psalm 107:10–16)

"Because they rebelled against God's commands and despised the plans of the Most High." Pesky little verse, that one. You may be thinking, *Thanks loads, Nigel—but how the heck could a person be rebellious when he or she was only a victim in all this?*

Well, in fact, when a person chooses to live with continued shame, bitterness, resentment, and unforgiveness resulting from the actions of another, they are rebelling against God's commands and His plans for their lives.

The intent of that verse is not to condemn us, but to make us cognizant of His love and plans for us to be, and live, at peace with others and ourselves! God did not make us victims. Nor are we condemned by the actions of our perpetrator(s) unless we refuse to obey God. In refusing to forgive, we literally hand over, to our perpetrator(s), control of our minds, bodies, and spirits. It's our choice. Ever heard the phrase "You made your bed, now lie in it"? Can we all agree that unforgiveness makes a most uncomfortable bed to lie in?

But wait, your supplicants shouldn't despair. There is yet good news! Look again at Psalm 107:13–14: "Then they cried to the LORD in their trouble, and he saved them from their distress. He brought them out of darkness, the utter darkness, and broke away their chains."

Friends, we do have the power and authority to consign ourselves to a prison cell by rebelling against God's commands and plans. But from that prison cell we can still cry out to Him and He will answer. He promised to never let go of us. But we must cry out to Him. He wants us to invite Him into our circumstances. Then, out of our obedience to Him, He rescues us.

Jesus came to set the captives free. That is still true to this very day!

You have the privilege of helping your supplicants imagine life without ever giving a second thought to their perpetrator(s)—a life free from that nasty gremlin stuck to their back, stealing their joy, using up all their energy, causing them to stoop, keeping them on high alert as they warily scan their world for persons or situations like those that scarred them. You can ask them to take a deep breath and ask the Lord to reboot their life without that parasite—to cry out to Him and be set free!

Your supplicants won't like what I am about to write now, but it is biblical. This truth has been a flashing neon light since Cain murdered his brother Abel. God has forgiven us in so many areas of our life. If we don't forgive others and our self, we are asserting ourselves over and above God! When we disobey His commands, we displace His authority and replace it with our own.

His command to forgive is abundantly clear. Just look at the following scriptures, all from the mouth of Jesus:

> Do not judge, and you will not be judged. Do not condemn, and you will not be condemned. Forgive, and you will be forgiven. (Luke 6:37)

> And when you stand praying, if you hold anything against anyone, forgive them, so that your Father in heaven may forgive you your sins. (Mark 11:25)

> But if you do not forgive others their sins, your Father will not forgive your sins. (Matthew 6:15)

Whoa, no wiggle room here. No parsing words, no twists or turns in interpretation. Flat out, if you don't forgive, you will not be forgiven. In the face of such straight talk from God, can anyone justify continued resistance to forgive?

In the face of such clear commands, why do we have such difficulty forgiving? Here are a few reasons I have heard over the years and what I say in response:

- "My perpetrator(s) are not repentant and have never asked me to forgive them."

  Sorry, but it matters not whether they have asked for your forgiveness. Your forgiveness of them is not for the purpose of being reconciled to them. In obeying Jesus, your forgiveness of them enables you to be reconciled to Jesus. Without your obedience, you are out of fellowship with your Savior. Therefore, your forgiveness is for your well-being and peace of mind, not theirs.

- "I don't feel like forgiving them. I have no feelings of kindness or goodwill toward them."

  Forgiveness is a decision; it is not about your feelings or anyone else's. Obedience to God does not wait for your feelings to conform to His command. There are only two Greek words in the New Testament that translate "forgive":

  - *Aphiemi* (forgive); literally means "to send away, to let go, to disregard, to leave, to depart from, to abandon." It is used 136 times in the New Testament and is the *only* word that Jesus used to address forgiveness.

  - *Charizomai* (forgive); literally means "to do a favor, to gratify, to give graciously, to show one's self gracious, kind, benevolent." It is used just nineteen times in the New Testament, but Jesus never used it in the context of forgiveness. He used it just once, in Luke 7:42, to demonstrate an *attitude* of grace.

    Jesus' choice of the word *aphiemi* commands our obedience to make a decision to leave behind, abandon, depart from, let go, send away: our pain, shame, bitterness, resentment, and hatred. *Aphiemi* emphasizes action and is devoid of feelings. Choose for yourself this day—life or death? Jesus knows best that there is life in forgiveness, but only death in unforgiveness.

- "My perpetrator(s) were so vile, they do not deserve to be forgiven."

Really? Sounds a bit like that servant who the king forgave a huge debt and then refused to forgive his fellow servant. This sentiment also resonates with my earlier warning that refusal to forgive asserts ourselves as above God. The Bible is clear—if we don't forgive, we cannot be forgiven! In the end, beloved, do any of us deserve to be forgiven? Definitely not. But thanks be to God, He paid the ultimate price to purchase the forgiveness of our sins for all time!

- "I haven't seen my perpetrator(s) and I don't want to; nor do I want to reconcile with them!"

Though they are not in your presence, your unforgiveness has joined you to your perpetrator(s). You can go nowhere without your pain, shame, bitterness, and resentment if you do not forgive them. It takes only two to forgive—just you and Jesus. You need not, nor should you, confront your offenders. Jesus' command to forgive your perpetrator(s) is not so you may be reconciled to them; rather it is so you may be restored and reconciled to Jesus! Beyond forgiveness, should Jesus ever lead you to so do, it takes three to reconcile—you, Jesus, and your perpetrator(s).

- "I know I should forgive, but when I try, I can't get past the memory of the wrong that was done to me."

At that very moment, recall instead how you came to know Jesus Christ as your Lord and Savior through the forgiveness of your sins. When you confessed, you were forgiven. The Lord took your sins to His cross. He died that you might have life abundantly. So, I must ask you: Is the sin of someone else robbing you of abundant life? The day you accepted Jesus as your

Lord and Savior, you asked, and He forgave your sins. Recall what you came to experience firsthand. Luke 1:77 says that Jesus came "to give his people the knowledge of salvation through the forgiveness of their sins." And Jesus explained to His disciples, as they were observing the first communion, "This is the blood of the covenant, which is poured out for many for the forgiveness of sins" (Matthew 26:28).

You have seen and tasted the goodness of God and His unfathomable love for you as He washed away your sins and clothed you with His robe of righteousness. No longer allow your unforgiveness of another's sins to steal your joy and cause you to fall prey to Jesus' warning in Matthew 7:2: "For in the same way you judge others, you will be judged, and with the measure you use, it will be measured to you."

Or is all this really just about you? Perhaps you need to forgive yourself. Doesn't the world beat up on us enough? If you are heaping self-condemnation upon yourself, I have two words for you: Stop yourself! Ask God to forgive you, and you will be free from that millstone around your neck and the dark cloud hovering over your head. If you believe Jesus to be who He said He is and to be the way, the truth, and the life, then read again from Romans 8:1: "Therefore, there is now no condemnation for those who are in Christ Jesus."

Did you know that we can also physically manifest this stubborn holding on to unforgiveness in our bodies? When supplicants present themselves complaining of neck pain, I've been known to inquire, "Who is the 'pain-in-the-neck' in your life?" That often leads to an unraveling of layers of unforgiveness and the need to forgive. It frequently happens that after we have unpacked the pain-in-the-neck, their pain clears up! The simplest matters that we've not forgiven can also trip us up (for example, forgiving the driver who rear-ended us or forgiving ourselves for running into someone else). I've heard it said that it takes a minute to find a special person, an hour to appreciate them, a day to love them, and then an entire lifetime to forgive them.

The following prayer has set many victims free. Encourage your supplicants who are struggling with forgiveness to say it out loud to God, even if their minds are fighting to stop them or they don't believe it is possible. God will hear their prayers! Tell them not to share this prayer with or notify those they need to forgive. This is between them and God only. This is their first step in breaking the power that their offenders have over them.

Lord, I forgive _____ (insert name of person or group) for the pain, shame, anger, and humiliation they have caused me. I forgive myself for all the time and energy I have expended in holding on to that pain and shame. Lord, I ask You to forgive _____ (insert name of person or group) for the pain and shame I have suffered. Please also forgive me for disobeying You by not forgiving them sooner. And I ask _____ (insert name of person or group) to also forgive me for all the anger and rage I've had against (him / her / them) for the pain (he / she / they) caused me.

You may also add:

Lord Jesus, it has been _____ (insert the number of years) since "The Incident." I don't want this millstone hanging around my neck any longer. I truly want to be set free—to be free indeed to have life abundantly. You promised to set the captives free and I have been held hostage for so many years. Lord, please set me free now to be able to live my life to the fullest.
Thank You, Jesus! Amen.

GENERATIONAL DAMAGE

*This is what you are to say to Joseph: I ask you
to forgive your brothers the sins and the wrongs
they committed in treating you so badly.*
—Genesis 50:17

We all inherit traditions, habits, beliefs, and behaviors passed down through the generations of our family lines. Some are positive and some are negative. Like Paul said in Philippians 4, we should dwell on whatever is good and worthy of praise. But as for those things that were clearly negative—well, friends, they need to go. We need to help our supplicants send them to Jesus to be healed. They need to be set free of them. They must break any cycles of racism, alcoholism, addictions, criminality, sorcery, witchcraft, depression, suicide, murder, or all other manner of ruin and evil, by surrendering all to Jesus and asking Him to cut them loose and heal their family lines for the sake of their prodigy. Why would we ever hang on to the deadwood in our family trees, if Jesus will cut it off and allow us to grow in freedom?

No doubt, many of the persons you will minister to were angered, embittered, or discouraged by their parents. They may not have forgiven them. Or they may have justified their parents' behavior by rationalizing that it was done for their own good. They may be misguidedly still trying to please or honor their parents by unwittingly (or perhaps intentionally) incorporating their negative behaviors, habits, traditions, or beliefs into their present lives. Perhaps they have even angered, embittered, or discouraged their own children and have not asked for their forgiveness.

Sometimes we excuse our learned behaviors, habits, beliefs, and traditions by taking comfort in their existence in our forbearers (parents, grandparents, uncles, aunts, and so on). Our need to justify those behaviors (et al.) can lead us to think, believe, and say aloud, "Just as my father did, so shall I . . ." I have dealt with this reality over and over in so many folks who have sought healing. "If _____ [for example, Dad or Mom] behaved that way, so can I!" Unfortunately, such justification continues to pass on and legitimize our foulest attributes, such as racism, misogyny, addictions, hatred, and aggression.

When our image of God as our heavenly Father is tainted by our earthly father's alcoholic, domineering, cantankerous, aggressive, angry, or _____ (you fill in the blank) behavior, it creates a personal need for healing—both inner and generational healing. Simply knowing that certain learned behaviors, traditions, beliefs, and habits have had a negative impact upon your life (and those who know and love you) will not purge them. They are embedded, often even hidden from conscious awareness. Asking God to heal you is a first step forward, but eventually it will be necessary to invite God's mercy, grace, and healing upon the past generations in your family tree.

I have a friend who is related to the infamous British highway robber Dick Turpin. Like Robin Hood, Turpin stole from the rich. Unlike Robin Hood, he kept the booty for himself. Whenever I see my friend, we fall out laughing as I dramatically clutch my pockets with both hands as he approaches. Though we can joke about this, consider that he is a direct descendant of a legendary thief and murderer who, at age thirty-three, was hanged for his crimes in England in 1739. Can you change the negative impact of your generational legacy? The answer is, definitively yes! Fortunately, with Christ's help, all things are possible. Just as my friend doesn't bear the stain of his infamous relative, we can also be set free.

The list of how the negativity of our forbearers impacts us is endless: divorce, adultery, violent or accidental death, infant death, miscarriage, abortion, unforgiveness, bitter root judgments, fear, anxiety, unresolved grief, physical illness, mental illness, physical abuse, sexual abuse, verbal abuse, suicide, satanic or occult activity, and addictions to food, alcohol, drugs, sex, work, and pornography. The adverse outcomes are devastating—and all may be passed on to us genetically or through "familiar or generational spirits." These spirits cling to us, and we pass them from generation to generation.

I remember the first time I heard myself repeat something, out of frustration, that I'd often heard my father say. I realized, then, that I was a mere clone and that family tradition is passed down in all its glory (or not) through our family lines. Yes, of course, among us are those blessed with idyllic childhoods. I would argue, though, that if the Lord sifted those, seemingly, more fortunate offspring, we'd likely find that their skeletons are just better hidden or that their skeletons were healed when another family member invited Jesus to heal their family lines.

More common are children whose parents did scar them, often unwittingly—by isolating from them, lying to them, being impatient with them, being critical of them, not listening to them, not talking to them, lacking interest in them, or other harmful behaviors. Perplexingly, upon occasion I've ministered to a sibling who came to me for healing from parental abuse—whose sibling maintains it never happened! This occurs because we are each unique and our perceptions are utterly personal. So, in the healing ministry, we must grasp what the late healing minister Fr. Al Durrance described in this way:

"Our perception is our reality, but it need not remain our actuality."[1] With Jesus Christ, we can transform our family history and help our supplicants transform theirs, with His-story!

Perhaps our elders told lies that, in our naiveté, have been handed down as truths. Here are a few misleading beliefs or traditions you and your supplicants may have heard as a child:

"Stop making faces like that. If the wind changes your face will stay that way!" "Stop crying or I'll give you something to cry about." "I brought you into this world, I can take you out." "Just wait till your father gets home." "Be sure to wear clean underwear in case you get in an accident!" "Shut your mouth and eat your supper." (Hmm, bit difficult to do . . .) "You will sit there until that plate is clean." "Eat your dinner—think of the starving people in China!" "Because I said so, that's why." "If I told you once, I've told you a million times . . ." "If you don't straighten up, I'm going to knock you into the middle of next week!" "If you fall out of that swing and break something, you're not going to the store with me." "Don't come crying to me if that lawn mower cuts off the toes of your bare feet!" "Millions of less fortunate children in this world would be more appreciative than you." "You better pray that will come out of my carpet." "You're just like your father (or other 'villain du jour')."

Though these clichés appear harmless and were likely not intended to do harm, they can still do damage.

What a time my friend had as an only child. In second grade, her parents told her that if she "failed" (anything less than an A), she'd be sent to a reformatory. Hours from home as her family drove to relatives in another state, she was terrified upon seeing the sign "Reform School for Girls." Hoping her parents didn't notice, she nearly fainted when her mother exclaimed, "There—that's where you're going if you fail!" She has memories of opening "failing" report cards and melting down as teachers tried to console her; of trying to forge her mother's signature on her cards; and, in high school, of considering suicide but not knowing how. As a mother, she became irate whenever she couldn't help her children understand how to do their homework. Though later healed by Jesus, only recently did she work out that the terrible stress she felt whenever she was unable to help with her children's homework was due to her implosive fear that they could fail!

It's possible that some of your supplicants have practiced these deceptions in an effort to control their own children. It probably didn't work, but it potentially may be damaging. Where did they learn them? Please understand this is not a guilt trip for parents. There are no perfect people, save Jesus Christ. But whenever beliefs, habits, traditions, and behaviors are recklessly perpetuated, without regard to origin or validity, they can cause a great deal of hardship and pain. Worse yet, we recycle and regurgitate them upon the next generation.

So far, I've shared about invisible damage done to our psyches and souls. Many of our scars are unseen. But some behaviors left unchecked in our families of origin are seen or made visible in our prodigy. The teen years are often emotionally turbulent, like an out-of-control roller coaster. Parents who try to take charge often encounter rigid pushback from willful teenagers. When strong will is pitted against strong will, the results are unpredictable and chaotic. Sadly, in some families, a tradition of punishment emerges. What we cannot control by word might best be controlled by force. When physical punishment is invoked, parents are often passing down habits used by their own parents. For whatever reason, they are duped into believing that "I survived, so will my children." But have we survived? Do our children survive? Is the word *survived* ever an appropriate description of our childhood and adolescent years?

I've also heard about "loving" punishment meted out by Christian parents. Until the late twentieth century, it was popularly held that disobedient children should be paddled or spanked. A disobedient child was sent to a designated place in the home (sometimes a stool) where they were to bend over and receive a swat on the bottom via a wooden paddle or bare hand. The hope was that the designated place would be perceived as a "love" seat where discipline was given with love, not anger. Sadly, upset by their child's behavior, in practice many parents had little success at maintaining a calm, loving demeanor while wielding their hand or other instrument across their child's backside. Consider that children who received such discipline, as they grew older, may have also experienced an escalation of discipline as their offenses were perceived as more grievous by their frenzied parents. At my boarding school a bamboo cane was used by my headmaster for discipline. It drew blood! Because I witnessed the effects, I only came close to being caned once.

In my experience, no matter how poorly parents expressed their love, I find that most truly do love their children. In healing, it is imperative for adults to revisit childhood wounds and be freed of them through forgiveness and inner healing. After being made aware of what was out of order in their lives, a next step might be to proactively seek generational healing—asking Christ to cut off anything harmful or evil from their past, preventing it from being replicated in future generations.

I am reminded of the story of an engineer at the fairground who observed a large elephant chained to a stake. The engineer was curious and commented to the elephant handler, "I say, that elephant is large enough to break his chain with just one pull of his hind leg." The handler replied, "Yes, indeed, but he doesn't know that. Elephants have incredible memories and when he tried, as a baby, to break his chain, he couldn't!"

There could be circumstances or wounds that are chaining your supplicants to the past. What do those chains do to their daily lives? Are they like the elephant—fooled by past words or actions that they believe to be accurate? Have those chains from their past beliefs, habits, traditions, or behaviors impacted them negatively? Have they been duped to believe they are unbreakable? Can you imagine helping them to reboot their lives and setting them free from generational burdens? What would their lives look like if all the negative baggage was dumped and they were set free?

If we are called as prayer ministers to help supplicants be freed from their burdens and negativity, we must listen, love, and pray. We must not interrupt, pry, manipulate, or add to their stories. We must not suggest or implant any line of thinking that is not generated first—and only—by the supplicant. Please know that it is illegal to implant a false memory in a supplicant, creating false memory syndrome. When ministering to a supplicant, let them tell their own story. They desperately need to be heard before their healing can begin. So, get out of the way!

It is also not your job to assess, confront, or challenge the memories of a supplicant. It is common for all of us to have inaccurate recollection or outright false memories of our past, but that will never impede Jesus' ministry of healing. We prayer ministers honor our supplicants by helping them to surrender their pain (real or imagined) to Jesus Christ so they can forgive those they believe perpetrated harm against them. Rest assured, dear brothers and sisters, Jesus will sort it all out in His time, not yours.

In the context of generational healing, supplicants often have uncorroborated suspicions of generational sin in their family lines. Many will complete genograms, based upon their personal belief that this, that, or the other occurred in their family lines. There is no harm in this because genograms are utterly confidential between Jesus and the supplicant. No other living person is to be made privy to the content of completed genograms. Let go and let God.

Generational healing, though not named as such in the Bible, can be found in many different scriptures. Remember Joseph's father's instructions before he died: "'This is what you are to say to Joseph: I ask you to forgive your brothers the sins and the wrongs they committed in treating you so badly.' Now please forgive the sins of the servants of the God of your father" (Genesis 50:17).

First Kings 15:3–4 implies generational sin and the need for healing: "He committed all the sins his father had done before him; his
heart was not fully devoted to the LORD his God, as the heart of David
his forefather had been. Nevertheless, for David's sake the LORD his
God gave him a lamp in Jerusalem by raising up a son to succeed him
and by making Jerusalem strong."

The entire chapter 28 of Deuteronomy sets forth the glorious blessings that await them and their offspring who obey God. Highlights of
those blessings are found in verses 1, 3–4: "The LORD your God will
set you high above all the nations on earth. . . . You will be blessed in
the city and blessed in the country. The fruit of your womb will be
blessed."

Conversely, however, in verses 15, 16, and 18, we read: "However,
if you do not obey the LORD your God . . . all these curses will come
on you and overtake you: You will be cursed in the city and cursed in
the country. . . . The fruit of your womb will be cursed."

I recommend reading all of Deuteronomy 28 as it might provide a spiritual awakening within you to seriously consider seeking
healing on behalf of your family lines. Are there any among us who
can attest, for certain, that every generation before us obeyed God?
Though some family members may have, it only takes one—even
you—to usher in the curses that follow those and their offspring who
disobey Him. Since it is more likely we all have generations that have
alternated between obedience and disobedience, shouldn't we all seek
generational healing?

As I have shared throughout this book, Jesus welcomes us to
bring all our hurts, wounds, and pain—whether emotional, physical,
or spiritual—to Him for His healing. Paul cautioned us to take care
how we live, not foolishly but wisely (Ephesians 5:15). We are warned
against squandering the grace that is ours in Christ, while the psalmist alluded to the surrender of our lives to Him for His scrutiny and
restoration: "Search me, God, and know my heart; test me and know

my anxious thoughts. See if there is any offensive way in me, and lead me in the way everlasting" (Psalm 139:23–24).

In truth, dear friend, this is just one of numerous invitations the Bible gives us to be healed, redeemed, restored, and regenerated while we are yet among the living. We don't have to live in uncertainty and pain; we need only surrender our lives to Him to examine and redeem. That, in a nutshell, is what generational healing is and does. And because of that healing we can "demolish arguments and every pretension that sets itself up against the knowledge of God, and we take captive every thought to make it obedient to Christ" (2 Corinthians 10:5). We can do this when we are bold to take back the ground that the enemy has stolen in our family lines.

How might you begin to help supplicants to surrender the generational sins of their family lines to Jesus Christ? It is far less complicated than you might think. But I want to say straight up that if you have questions or are lacking local resources (for example, finding a healing ministry), please contact my ministry online at: www.byhiswoundsministry.org, and we'll do our best to give you some direction. Now let's begin:

1. Ask supplicants to invite Jesus to be present with them and listen to Him, as He is their Healer. Jesus will advise them on a need-to-know basis—He will only show them what is essential for them to know *now* at this point in their healing journey.
2. Share with the supplicants what has been written elsewhere in this book on the Holy Spirit (i.e., the baptisms of, the gifts and fruits of the Holy Spirit). Go slow. Have them pray for Jesus to release in them every gift and fruit they'll need to create a safe place to better understand the past.
3. Help them find a Christian healing ministry. Inquire whether the church or group offers generational healing. Their best

prospects are churches or ministries that don't require member-ship or charge fees (though donations are welcome). Suggest that, as they discover new-to-you aspects of Jesus' nature, they don't hastily leave their home church. Jesus may yet need them there.

4. The work your supplicant will do in the above steps will prepare them to prayerfully complete a genogram (notable problems within a family tree). A sample genogram, created by a friend, is found on my website: www.byhiswoundsministry.org. If you prefer another form, go for it! In any event, your suppli-cants should *be aware* of the following caveats concerning the completion of genograms:

– A genogram is not a collaborative effort. It is a solo pursuit by you with Jesus' help. Do not call upon family members to discuss or quiz them about suspected areas of notable problems. And do not discuss or share your work with your spouse, parents, siblings, or children. This is for only you and Jesus!

– Do not fret over whether your suspicions of notable problems are accurate or not—Jesus knows, and He will accurately heal your perceived concerns.

– Do not keep your notes or copies of the finished genogram—nor commit it to memory. When completed, seal it in a plain envelope and surrender it to Jesus during a service that is often called a Litany for Generational Healing. Burning the genogram, offering the smoke as incense and committing the ashes as dust to dust, is also acceptable.

– It's entirely possible that as the Lord continues to heal you He may reveal more information about your family lines in the years ahead. Should that occur, simply redo this exercise until you have His peace.

5. At this point in a supplicant's generational healing journey, I often suggest the person participate in the Litany for Generational Healing. Details concerning this service are not in this book because it is best *not* to proceed alone. This service of healing is typically conducted by clergy or lay leaders with experience in this area of healing ministry. They will use a litany or other order of service of their choosing. Though this service can be celebrated for one person, it is particularly holy when you are joined by others also seeking healing for their family lines. Though the content of your genogram remains confidential, all who gather stand in the gap for their families—renouncing all evil, including satanic, occult, and new age practices, and asking God's forgiveness and redemption for past, present, and future generations.

6. During the litany, completed genograms may be placed on the altar or Lord's Table. It is preferable and a great blessing to also celebrate the Eucharist (Holy Communion or the Lord's Supper) within this service. At the conclusion of the litany, the clergy or lay leader may gather all the genograms and burn them in a fireplace or suitable receptacle out of doors. All are welcome to witness this burning—praying, praising, and rejoicing for the healing and freedom that Jesus earned for us by His wounds.

A service for generational healing is one of my favorite celebrations. It is my experience that the presence of the Lord is palpable as we humbly and reverently gather to confess, repent, and ask God's forgiveness for our families' generational sins. Those who have participated and witnessed the burning of their genograms (documents heavily laden with the burdens and cares of this world) attest to feeling a sense of joy, relief, and exquisite freedom. Just brilliant! My fellow clergy and lay leaders have also shared that for them each burning is extraordinary and unique—even in the fearsome way those papers ignite and burn! Flames have leapt to great heights, while at other times they smolder and burn slowly. Smoke can be thick and black or nearly smokeless. Some papers turn black and vanish, while others turn white and gracefully float away. It is never the same. Each of us is fearfully and wonderfully made—all are loved and adored the same and yet are splendidly unique in Him.

Know that the Lord is merciful and eager to shower your suppliants with His most abundant blessings. He desires them to be healed, made whole and ready to become colaborers on earth and heirs in His kingdom. For them to become all that He designed them to be, they must first receive and accept His unfathomable love and His greatest gifts. This will likely require their own healing and, in due course, the healing of their family lines. As they are made aware of their need for healing, I pray that generational healing will be part of their journey.

I often find myself quoting, "Of course your family pushes your buttons, they installed them!" Generational healing rewires the connections.

Lord, in Your mercy hear our fervent prayers for Your healing of our families—past, present, and future generations! All glory and honor to You, Lord Christ! Alleluia! Alleluia! Amen!

PAINFUL MEMORIES

*Then you will know the truth, and
the truth will set you free.*
—John 8:32

In the gospel of Matthew, we are told that Jesus was arrested and Peter waited in the courtyard of the high priest Caiaphas. A servant girl asked if he was with Jesus, but Peter pretended he didn't know what she was talking about. A second time, another servant girl accused him before the whole crowd as having been with Jesus, but Peter denied knowing Him. Finally, others in the crowd began to confront him, insisting that he had been with Jesus, even adding that his "accent gives [him] away" (Matthew 26:73). This third time Peter became agitated. Matthew 26:74–75 records: "Then he [Peter] began to call down curses, and he swore to them, 'I don't know the man!' Immediately a rooster crowed. Then Peter remembered the word Jesus had spoken: 'Before the rooster crows, you will disown me three times.' And he went outside and wept bitterly."

Peter melted down. Can you imagine his horror—denying Jesus? He had just done the very thing he'd sworn he would never do! Having spent three years with Jesus, he had waited in Caiaphas's courtyard, hoping to catch a glimpse of Him or get news of His condition. Caught in that difficult situation, Peter chose to lie and deny his love for Christ. I find it very easy to put myself in his sandals. One can only imagine the flood of anxiety, fear, and confusion that was pulsating through his every cell. Whether out of fear or to self-protect, Peter denied Christ three times.

And then Jesus was crucified.

We don't catch up with Peter again in Matthew's account until after Jesus is resurrected (though Luke 24 and John 20 both record that Peter ran to Jesus' tomb when he learned it was empty). The women who discovered the empty tomb had also encountered the risen Christ and obeyed His request to tell the remaining disciples to meet Him in Galilee (Matthew 28:5–10), which they did (v. 16).

From John 21 we learn that the redemption of Peter's shame came several days, or even a week or more, later when the disciples gathered at the Sea of Galilee and went fishing. Since Jesus had sent word to them to return to Galilee, it is much to their credit that they did as He asked and remained there until He revealed Himself to them. The disciples fished all night long, to no avail. In the early morning, while yet in their boat a hundred yards or so from land, a man called out from the shore instructing them to throw their net to the right of their boat—and instantly the net was teeming with 153 fish! It was John who first declared that the man was Jesus, but it was Peter who leapt out of that boat, into the water, to go to Jesus on shore.

When the boat carrying the other disciples arrived, Jesus was already cooking fish and bread over hot coals. Jesus invited them all to breakfast. When the Lord asked that they bring some of their fresh catch to cook also, Peter promptly returned to the boat to retrieve the bulging net filled with fish. I imagine this was Peter's effort to begin to reclaim Jesus' favor after his betrayal. I think I would have also offered to shine His sandals while I was at it, wouldn't you?

John 21 describes, in detail, how Jesus healed Peter's guilt and shame of the betrayal. It is a stunning illustration of Jesus Christ methodically revisiting the deep wound within Peter, just one more time, by insinuating Himself in the midst of the memory and leading Peter through his total healing of that memory. The New International Version titles the passage below "Jesus Reinstates Peter."

> When they had finished eating, Jesus said to Simon Peter, "Simon son of John, do you love me more than these?"
>
> "Yes, Lord," he said, "You know that I love you."
>
> Jesus said, "Feed my lambs."
>
> Again Jesus said, "Simon son of John, do you love me?"
>
> He answered, "Yes, Lord, you know that I love you."
>
> Jesus said, "Take care of my sheep."
>
> The third time he said to him, "Simon son of John, do you love me?"
>
> Peter was hurt because Jesus asked him the third time, "Do you love me?" He said, "Lord, you know all things; you know that I love you."
>
> Jesus said, "Feed my sheep. Very truly I tell you, when you were younger you dressed yourself and went where you wanted; but when you are old you will stretch out your hands, and someone else will dress you and lead you where you do not want to go." Jesus said this to indicate the kind of death by which Peter would glorify God. Then he said to him, "Follow me!" (John 21:15–19)

Peter had denied knowing Jesus Christ three times, and now the Lord was giving him this opportunity to be set free of his heavy burden of guilt and shame by asking him three times, "Do you love me?" Jesus was healing Peter's memory . . . reframing the shame, guilt, emotional pain, and self-condemnation he had felt when he betrayed Christ. All of us, including our supplicants, have memories like this. Not one of us is without circumstances or events in this life that produced despair, grief, regret, shame, pain, or guilt. Is this resonating with your spirit right now? Can you relate to Peter in your own situation? Do you cringe and feel great shame when you recall it? Be assured that your supplicants will too.

Three times Peter denied Jesus. Three times he betrayed Christ, violating his own pledge that he would *never* forsake his Lord. And yet, he had! To heal Peter, Jesus accompanied him back through his three blatant denials, by eliciting from him three declarations of love for Him.

FIRST DENIAL: "I don't know what you are talking about."
FIRST DECLARATION: "Yes, Lord, You know that I love You."

SECOND DENIAL: "I don't know the man!"
SECOND DECLARATION: "Yes, Lord, You know that I love You."

THIRD DENIAL: While calling down curses, he swore, "I don't know the man!"
THIRD DECLARATION: *"Lord, You know all things; You know that I love You."*

The only word that comes to my mind here is *brilliant*. Thanks be to God for our Jesus!

You see, whenever we do something that we regret or when someone has done something painful to us, we become haunted. We are broken and filled with shame, and sometimes we even become embittered and resentful—whether we sinned against ourselves or someone sinned against us. Memories can be a "plague on our houses" as they fester, infect, disturb, agitate, contaminate, possess, pollute, and inflame our lives. Negative responses to memories cause us to fixate and obsess on them until they control how we perceive the world around us, including ourselves and all who remind us of those who have sinned against us.

This book is being penned in the midst of what has been dubbed the #MeToo movement, comprised of people who have felt abused verbally, physically, or sexually. The problem with the #MeToo phenomenon is that there is no healing in simply declaring victimhood! In fact, the goal of this group is to indict their perpetrators and see that they are publicly disgraced, if not ruined in their future lives. But the natural flesh response of perpetrators, when indicted, is utterly human—they deny, defend, or justify their actions. Had Peter attempted to defend or justify his behavior, could Jesus have been successful in reinstating Peter to serve Him? No, of course not! Consumed with the need to self-defend and self-preserve, the path of repentance may be narrowed or even closed. But if perpetrators are forgiven, in and through the love of Christ, they are disarmed. It may even become possible for them to acknowledge their heinous deeds and seek restitution.

In John 21, Jesus disarmed the guilt and shame that filled Peter in the wake of that tragic night in the courtyard. Jesus pulled all residual toxicity out of Peter's soul, by its root, and planted His unfailing love in the void! Jesus' love for Peter—His ability to manifest the forgiveness He earned for him and all of us on the cross in His dying and out of His resurrection—has more power than any wounding memories we might have. This is "the healing of memories" or "inner healing," that every human being requires 24/7, 52/365. None of us have yet arrived, even when we know this; but all who believe Jesus Christ as their Lord and Savior are on the way.

You goal as a minister of healing is to help supplicants not allow their past to ruin their present or future. To keep them from handing over boundless power to an offender, whether in their past or present life. If they wallow in self-pity, they will only deepen their wound like a stuck needle engraves an old LP vinyl record.

Here is the rub: because of His gift of free will to us, God does not stop airplanes from crashing into commercial buildings, nor does He not cause a rapist to drop dead in the midst of an assault. The same free will that allows us to choose to obey and choose to worship Him, as followers of Jesus, is the same free will that keeps Him from interfering when an inebriated driver causes an accident. God does not interfere with free will. We humans have been given the freedom to choose whether we will love one another or visit reckless and painful behavior upon one another. This, of course, does not mean that God is oblivious to the pain that our free will, less-than-best choices, produce.

Sadly, many of us have squandered our free will and fallen far away from His command to love our neighbors as ourselves. The saying that now comes to my mind is one we frequently hear at Christmastime: "Peace on earth and goodwill to mankind." But, in truth, man is not always kind . . . oh, that there truly were peace and goodwill among man-unkind! It is totally heartbreaking to sit with souls, wounded by man-unkind, who frequent my office every day. We humans can be so utterly cruel to one another—and not just those who are lost. Believers can be equally cruel in their behavior whenever they are unfaithful to the God they claim to believe.

How can we be set free from such haunting memories? Jesus made it very clear: "Surely I am with you always, to the very end of the age" (Matthew 28:20). Hebrews restates this promise of our Lord: "God has said, 'Never will I leave you; never will I forsake you.' So we say with confidence, 'The Lord is my helper; I will not be afraid. What can mere mortals do to me?'" (13:5–6).

As you begin the healing of memories ministry with a supplicant, keep in mind the twin sinister culprits that often follow a person's most hurtful incidents that were perpetrated by others'—or, in some instances, by their own—doing. They will dog a person, exhausting their energy and robbing their contentment and joy. Over the years I have ministered to some suffering souls who felt totally condemned by God, in—shall we say—an Old Testament manner. Frankly, many Christians are genuinely misguided folks, so strictly fundamentalist in their view of God, that they completely *mis*understand His nature, His Word, and His mission. Consequently, when I encounter such conflicted souls, I find them buried under mountains of guilt and shame.

We must help our supplicants navigate through their propensity to self-condemn. In my office, several times each week, I revisit Romans 8:1: "Therefore, there is now no condemnation for those who are in Christ Jesus." Please stop reading right now and ponder what I have just written. I must ask: Who is condemning us? Who is telling us that we are not worthy? Who is stealing our joy? Can we not see that when we surrendered our lives to Christ and asked His forgiveness, any belief that He would now condemn us is a lie from the pit of hell? Paul said so in Romans 8:1! There is no condemnation for we who are in Christ. We must believe it is so and forgive ourselves.

And yet, many of those with whom we minister struggle at just this point. They have memories that trouble them and that have become blocks to living their lives to the fullest. What baggage can you help them discover that needs to be unpacked so that they may dispose of all that impedes their freedom in Christ? What strongholds or bondage is robbing them of the abundant life that Christ died to give them?

Our supplicants need to know they are beloved by the One who knows them best and loves them most, Jesus Christ Himself! There is nothing, absolutely nothing too difficult for Jesus. How can they be so sure that those strongholds will go when they decide to be rid of them? Because Paul wrote to the believers in Corinth and told them exactly what they have been given in Christ to win their freedom:

> The weapons we fight with are not the weapons of the world. On the contrary, they have divine power to demolish strongholds. We demolish arguments and every pretension that sets itself up against

the knowledge of God, and we take captive every thought to make it obedient to Christ. And we will be ready to punish every act of disobedience, once your obedience is complete. (2 Corinthians 10:4–6)

If a person has accepted Jesus as their Lord and Savior, confessed their offenses to Him, asked His forgiveness, come boldly before His throne of grace, and asked Him to fill them with His Holy Spirit and all His itinerant gifts and fruit, then their old mind is being regenerated. With His Spirit, they are also being empowered to overcome and defeat every stronghold that they have put upon themselves or that has been imposed upon them by others. In surrendering every thought or feeling, purposing themselves to demolish all arguments and pretenses that distort God's truth, and making their every thought or impulse obedient to Jesus, their obedience will be complete and their freedom will be defended by Christ.

I want to further highlight 2 Corinthians 10:5—"We demolish arguments and every pretension that sets itself up against the knowledge of God, and we take captive every thought to make it obedient to Christ"—because this passage is such a jewel in Christ's ministry to free the captives. Whether a person has experienced trauma related to physical, emotional, or sexual abuse, this verse is pivotal in the ministry of inner healing. Take captive every thought and memory and make it obedient to Christ. Take all the accumulated pain and surrender it all to Jesus. No, they do not get erased, but because they are a part of a believer, God will recycle them to work for them and not against them in the future. If ever those memories should dare revisit, they will have been neutralized. Their negativity will be gone, and they will no longer be able to trigger shame and guilt.

In the process of healing memories, I envision Jesus taking possession of a DVD that is loaded with recordings of a supplicant's memories. Before Jesus arrived on the scene, the DVD could interrupt their peace at any time or place of its choosing, instantly giving rise and import to the memories of troubling events. Pity parties might also spontaneously burst forth at those times. But after Jesus takes possession of that DVD and is permitted by them to remove it from "its player," the Lord then authoritatively stamps the word *healed* across every single frame of those memories. (Don't forget to invite Jesus to your pity party!)

How can this be? Though there may be vivid, framed images of memories, there is no set script to follow. Our faith in Christ, and the assurance we have of His Holy Spirit, will cast off all the former hauntings and provide people with every resource they'll need to retrieve, surrender, and reframe every harmful memory stuck in their hearts and minds. Let's look at how Christ's redemption can be achieved.

First, we'll begin with where the preferred location might be for doing this ministry. Though there is no right or wrong place, it must be safe, simple, and quiet—silence is optimal. With that in mind, let's look also at who needs to be present during this ministry. Of course, we will need one or two healing prayer ministers (no more unless necessary) and Jesus! When you gather to minister, be sure to pray for Jesus' presence to be palpably known to the supplicant, inviting the Holy Spirit to freely share the gifts that He has at His disposal. Ask the Lord to tether your supplicant to His cross—and to guard, defend, and protect them as you proceed.

As you enter in, encourage the supplicant to tell their story, taking the time they need (within reason), allowing them to provide as much detail as possible without including the most graphic details about their rape, molestation, injury, or whatever the case may be. Stop the "DVD player" just before those graphics, unless the supplicant indicates that something within the graphics is essential. With the "video paused," gently invite the supplicant to close their eyes and look around, in their mind's eye, for Jesus. He could be anywhere (inside, outside, looking through a window, behind them). Do not proceed until after they have invited Him in and they either see Him or feel His presence. Wait on the Lord. You may also elect not to lay hands upon the supplicant at any time during Christ's personal ministry to them. There is no need when Jesus Himself is there. When they confirm His presence, you might ask them to describe what Jesus is doing (for example, looking at them, speaking to them, touching them). While Christ reveals Himself to them, their memories are being "reframed" by His powerful presence.

Some healing ministers, through the empowerment of the Holy Spirit, may be silently given a "parallel" vision, which allows them to see in their mind's eye what the supplicant is seeing. If this happens, it is usually to help the supplicant experience His presence, but certainly not to direct the supplicant. Many times, supplicants see Jesus physically holding them, or feel Him or see just His hand. Many see the Lord weeping within the scene in the supplicant's memory. If they have difficulty, knowing Scripture is helpful to quote and reassure that He is with us always. He promised to never leave or forsake us. He is our healer, provider, and comforter.

This is a very delicate time. Do not rush, do not ask any questions unless the Lord prompts you, and don't interrupt in general. In her doctoral work on healing, the Rev. Valerie Balius, an Anglican clergy, found that supplicants who see, hear, or feel the presence of Christ during the healing of memories are totally and completely set free. When supplicants themselves experience Jesus during their memories, those memories are reframed. When healing ministers insinuate themselves into this sacred time, the fruit of any healing is often short-lived. I often put my hand over my mouth to keep myself silent.

Know that Christ's Spirit, within you, is holding a soul in your "hand" during this time. It is a sacred time He gives us to witness His healing of a broken child of God. As He sets the captive free, the air is almost electric, the space is thick with His presence; even the healing minister is uplifted as the Holy Spirit washes over the past horrors the supplicant suffered. The supplicant may sit quietly, showing no effect, remaining still. Or they may weep, usually not sobbing. If they emote in agony, do not touch them—but you may pray aloud for Jesus to affirm He is truly present, loving and healing them. If tears flow and noses run, simply slip a tissue into their hands, allowing them to remain in that moment with Christ.

As I mentioned before, healing minister Fr. Al Durrance was fond of saying, "Your perception may be your reality, but it need not remain your actuality." With Christ present, these painful memories are reframed and redeemed. The perception once held as reality by the supplicant is changed and their actuality is expanded to include Jesus Christ's healing of their memories. Where fear once pounded on their door, faith now answers, and no one is there!

I never cease to be amazed at what God does in the healing of memories. It is so humbling and beautiful—such a privilege—to see people surrender their soul wounds, and be set free in an instant by their Savior and Lord. I have hundreds of stories of people being set free from every imaginable situation or circumstance. The following is just one illustration.

No two sessions of healing are alike, especially with inner healing. Nor are supplicants alike. Where one is ready, willing, and able to take hold of Jesus as He overcomes and reframes their painful memories, others are not so simple to work with. Engineers, for instance, can be rather difficult to pray for. They live and move and have their beings—all in their heads! I once ministered to a British engineer (double trouble!) who had been rejected by his family after deciding (really, agreeing with the hospital's recommendation) to sign a document authorizing his mother's life support to be disconnected. She was brain dead, and the doctors were adamant that she could not be restored to the living. The rest of his family, however, could not bear this to be done. They convinced themselves she would be well again.

This man had not only lost his mum, but his entire family rejected him for signing that form. He was consumed with grief.

We walked through that memory, replaying that video, if you will. We paused the DVD at the very moment his mum stopped breathing. I asked him to look for Jesus in the room. He could not see Him. He kept looking. Nothing. After quite some time, I heard myself humming the tune of "Open the Eyes of My Heart," a popular contemporary praise and worship song. I was then led to instruct him to stop looking with his mind and let his heart search for the Lord's presence. Immediately, this man saw Jesus, but not with his mother at her death.

He shared that "she is already in heaven and being looked after by the Lord." Then he looked to the right and then to the floor and said aloud, "I see Him with my sister." He went on to describe his sister on the floor in a fetal position, sobbing in her grief. He said Jesus was on His knees ministering to her. His whole countenance changed as a smile eclipsed his face. It was such an honor to watch as the Lord set this man free. Weeks later, he let me know that this whole memory had been reframed and "now, every time I recall turning off the life support for Mum, I see Jesus!"

Inner healing is a process through which painful and traumatic memories are taken captive and made obedient to Christ. But John 8:32 says: "Then you will know the truth, and the truth will set you free." The truth is that God will never leave us or forsake us and that He is with us always. The truth is also that something may have happened in the past that violated you in some way. Such memories morph and reshape us, leaving us with a false identity. We then begin to live under the shadow of invisible scare (scar) tissue, only made visible by irregular conduct. Painful memories leach into our thinking and give rise to pain-producing behaviors (for example, isolation, anger, short fuses, and self-medications [alcohol or drugs], necessary to numb the pain).

Trauma does not define you, nor does PTS. The Lord needs us to stand strong in our faith in Him and believe Him when He tells us that we are not irretrievably broken. We are not hopeless, and we are certainly not helpless. He wants us to know that we were not made to live this way. "The one who calls you is faithful, and he will do it" (1 Thessalonians 5:24). If we are slaves, then let us be thus to Christ—not to some trumped-up accusatory memories, perpetrated by those who oppressed us. Those allegations are silenced in the presence of Jesus Christ. Perpetrators' threats to harm our families, or our pets, if ever we tell someone what was done to us are without substance. Their power has no standing before Jesus Christ. Before Him, you are safe. He is faithful, and He will do it! Let us not limit God in our estimation of what He can do. Let's boldly surrender our wounded memories and allow Jesus to be our Healer.

We have learned from the military and other investigatory organizations that a Critical Incident Debriefing (CID) completed as soon as possible after the occurrence of a traumatic event is the best defense against troubling memories. The closer in time the debriefing takes place, the less power its memory will have in the future. Ideally, suppliants should seek out healing soon after trauma occurs. I am thrilled at a new trend I have been seeing over the past twenty or so years. Parents are boldly bringing their sons and daughters to receive inner healing much sooner after they are harmed. Considering how menacing childhood memories can be, I am overjoyed that savvy parents are beating the enemy at his game—stopping trauma from playing havoc on their children by delaying healing. That said, let's not forget that time is firmly in the hands of God. Do not be afraid if you think it is too late. Do not waste time admonishing yourself if you have delayed your healing. God is faithful, and whenever you humbly call upon Him, He will answer you in your need.

Note: Do not attempt to pattern the healing of memories or inner healing by employing this book as a prescriptive or manual of how to proceed. Healing ministers require discernment and oversight by experienced ordained ministers and laypersons who can prescribe safe protocols to follow. Before diving into inner healing, it is best to spend time helping supplicants to understand who they are in Christ and walking them through important areas, such as forgiveness. Please don't let your past ruin your present or your future.

A Supplicant's Prayer

Lord Jesus, please free me from the haunting memories that plague my life. Please stand between those memories and me, between the hurtful incidents and me, and between the perpetrator(s) and me. I feel such guilt and deep shame and have difficulty believing that I can be forgiven. Your Word says there is no condemnation in You and asks me to seek first the kingdom of God. Help me to believe and obey You, Jesus. Help me to forgive myself as well as those who have sinned against me. Lord, help me to take captive my thoughts, fears, bitterness, and self-condemnation and make them obedient to You. I surrender all of myself to You and ask all that You are to overcome the pain and the scars of my heart and mind. Thank You, Jesus, for unraveling my memories and setting me free from all that binds and tethers me to the past. Lord, thank You for the gift of Your life that allows me to live life to the fullest, this day and every day in the future. In Your most Holy Name, Amen.

Grace and peace be with you, always, dear souls.

CONCLUSION

Because you know that the testing of
your faith develops perseverance.
—JAMES 1:3

fter Jesus prayed for a blind man, He asked him, "Do you see anything?" The man responded, "I see trees as men walking" (Mark 8:22–26). Jesus didn't hesitate; He knew that healing had begun, but it just wasn't yet complete. Immediately He prayed a second time. Even Jesus prayed twice for a stubborn healing need. This says to me that we need to press on and persevere as ministers of healing in this broken world. *Lord, I believe—in confidence and abounding faith even in the face of what may seem hopeless—Lord, I believe!*

Yet, I confess that sometimes I need a rest. I know when it gets to that point, my spirit is out of joint. Juxtaposed with a ministry of healing, if I know that only Jesus heals, then why should I need a rest? If I am feeling burdened by my supplicants' stories, then I have taken on things Christ never asked me nor wanted me to do. And why would He? He does not need you or me to heal anyone; He simply calls us to make ourselves available to be used as His hands in healing prayer. After we answer His call, it is Jesus who does all the work necessary to heal the hurting ones for whom we pray.

What is God saying to us about our call to healing ministry? Very simply, we must press on! Press on! Press on! Press on! What prize am I looking forward to? Ah, to hear Him say the words: "Well done, good and faithful servant."

As we press on and persevere, it is important to seek first the kingdom of God. We need to be aware that in our humanness our faith will wax and wane, ebb and flow. Sometimes we will have spiritual highs and other times spiritual lows. We might even encounter the dark night of the soul. But regardless of our circumstances, we must obey Him and trust Him to get us through, no matter what it takes.

We must not be put off by how things appear. We must remain expectant. Mark 8:25 says that "once more" Jesus put His hands on the blind man's eyes. Even Jesus persevered; He prayed again. The words *once more* leap off the page in this reading. How many "once more" opportunities will we have in our lives? Lord willing, plenty of them.

My mentor Francis MacNutt asked me in 1981, "Nigel, are you in this for the sprint or the long haul?" I told him that because of what I had seen God do in my sister's (Julie Mumford Sheldon) miraculous healing from dystonia, I wanted to give glory to God, so, my answer remains, "I am in this for the long haul." If I am in this for the long haul, I anticipate many more instances where I will pray "once more." As a healing minister, I commit myself to the long haul and will expectantly pray "once more," until the evidence of His healing is made manifest. As a Brit, I can hear the words of our beloved prime minister Sir Winston Churchill admonish us, "Never, never give up!"

Never giving up is more than just a waiting game. Beyond the "once mores" are other ways in which we train ourselves to persevere. One is to take captive our perspective and surrender it to Him. The words of my friend J. John, who graciously wrote the foreword to this book, come to mind. Regarding David slaying Goliath, he said that David could have responded in one of two ways when he first saw Goliath: "Oh no! He's really big, I better run away!" or "Oh, he's really big . . . how can I miss?" Likewise, the Lord's perspective allows us to press on in prayer. We must always see our supplicants through the eyes of Jesus. Any other perspective can discourage a healing prayer minister's faith in Christ for healing.

Another attribute that abides in healing ministers is peace. His peace. Remember that Jesus' peace passes all understanding. Regardless of how big your mountain is, take hold of His peace so that you can faithfully ask Jesus to move it! Psalm 23:2 says, "He makes me lie down in green pastures, he leads me beside quiet waters." The imagery of how the shepherd leads his flock to still water is so powerful. The anatomy of sheep is that their noses and mouths are located very close together. To prevent the sheep from getting water up their noses, the shepherd finds water that is not agitated. Still waters provide the optimal way for the sheep to drink and satisfy their thirst. Likewise, we want to shepherd our supplicants to a place of peace for their healing. Simply bringing peace to supplicants is in itself a healing experience.

I come to the end of this book and share with you the words of St. Ignatius of Loyola—a prayer that was recited by my entire school, daily, at nine in the morning during assembly. I said this prayer from ages five to seven—three years, five times each week, or 780 times in my life! This prayer has followed me all my life. I am especially fond of the line "to labor and not to seek *reward*."

Dear Lord Jesus Christ,
    Teach me to be generous;
    Teach me to serve You as You deserve,
    To give, and not to count the cost,
    To fight, and not to heed the wounds,
    To toil, and not to seek for rest,
    To labor, and not to seek reward,
    Except that of knowing that I do Your will.
Amen.

My dear brothers and sisters—my fellow healing ministers—do press on! Persevere and keep your eyes upon Jesus. Never forget how loved you are by the Lord. May His resurrection power be upon you for your healing as well as those for whom you pray.

Be well, do good works, and for the sake of God, love one another. Amen.

ACKNOWLEDGMENTS

My true heartfelt thanks:

To the late Canon Jim Glennon, who started me on this amazing journey.

To Cindi Scholander, who helped me mold my words from the rough clay of my mind into fine china. You are patient, understanding, and an amazing wordsmith.

To every person I have prayed with who unwittingly taught me how to pray for the next person over the past thirty years. Indeed, our adversities are God's universities!

To my personal prayer team . . . you know who you are, thank you, dear souls.

To The Rev. Dr. Andrew Buchanan, the prayer team, and parishioners of Galilee church, Virginia Beach, who have supported and encouraged me in this ministry.

To my dear friend The Rev. Canon J. John, a powerhouse of positive Christian perspective and weekly prayer support.

To all at HarperCollins who have made this publishing journey a pleasant and amazing experience.

To my dear wife, Lynn, who has stood by me for many years as the ministry grew and also endured my getting up at 4:00 most mornings to write this book. Thank you for your silent encouragement and extraordinary patience.

To Jesus, who commanded His disciples to "preach the Kingdom and heal the sick" (Luke 9:2). Thank you, Sir, for my marching orders for the past thirty years. To God for allowing me to work in His vineyard and to see the work of His hands on a daily basis. For Yours, Lord, is the Power and the Glory . . . All the Glory goes to you Lord, my Rock and my Salvation.

NOTES

Chapter 5: Courage

1. W. Ryan Rebold, *Nothing but Faith in My Pocket: A Journey off the Pew and into the World* (Mustang, OK: Tate Publishing, 2011), 53.
2. Bobby Styles, "Wizard of Oz: If I Were the King of the Forest," YouTube (video), June 3, 2011, https://youtu.be/gOCNY9pJ850.

Chapter 8: Faith

1. Jim Glennon, *Your Healing Is Within You* (Alachua, FL: Bridge-Logos, 1978), 30.

Chapter 9: Desire

1. Tom Mann, *Do You Want to Be Healed? Allowing God to Heal Brokenness in Your Life* (Maitland, FL: Xulon Press, 2013).

Chapter 11: Unanswered Prayer

1. Oswald Chambers, *My Utmost for His Highest*.
2. Chambers, *My Utmost for His Highest*.

Chapter 14: Unworthiness and Low Self-Esteem

1. C. S. Lewis, *The World's Last Night and Other Essays* (NY: Harcourt).

Chapter 15: Guilt and Shame

1. "Guilt," *Psychology Today*, https://www.psychologytoday.com/us/basics/guilt.

2. Philip Yancey, "Guilt Good and Bad," *Christianity Today*, November 18, 2002, https://www.christianitytoday.com/ct/2002/november18/36.112.html.

3. Yancey, "Guilt Good and Bad."

4. Cathy L. Grossman, "'Catholic Guilt,' 'Jewish Guilt' not Just a Joke, It's Essential," *USA Today*, October 14, 2010, http://usatoday30.usatoday.com/news/religion/2010-09-11-guilt14ONLINE_ST_N.htm.

5. "Guilt," *Psychology Today*, https://www.psychologytoday.com/us/basics/guilt.

6. Mary C. Lamia, PhD, "Shame: A Concealed, Contagious, and Dangerous Emotion," *Psychology Today*, April 4, 2011, https://www.psychologytoday.com/us/blog/intense-emotions-and-strong-feelings/201104/shame-concealed-contagious-and-dangerous-emotion.

7. Lamia, "Shame."

8. Rowan Williams, "The Radical Hospitality of Jesus," *Anglican Journal* 140, no. 9, November 2014, https://www.questia.com/magazine/1G1-390323519/the-radical-hospitality-of-jesus.

Chapter 16: Unforgiveness

1. Tim Teeman, our last interview.

2. ABC/20/20 Season 25 Episode 34, Air date: August 6, 2004, broadcast of interview of Joan Rivers: "Metacritic TV Episode Reviews, Aug. 6, 2004, Bob Brown interviews comic and red-carpet host Joan Rivers." Story found in Cindi Scholander's weekly devotional *Parting Thoughts*.

Chapter 17: Generational Damage

1. Verbal history. This was Fr. Al Durrance's signature quote. Fr. Durrance rarely wrote; when he did it was for notes in class. I heard him say this many times.

ABOUT THE AUTHOR

The Reverend Nigel Mumford is an international speaker, author, and founder of By His Wounds, Inc., a nonprofit organization focused on Christian healing. Nigel is also Priest Associate for Prayer Ministry at Galilee Church in Virginia Beach, Virginia.

Born and educated in England, Nigel served for six and a half years in Her Majesty's Royal Marine Commandos. Nigel has been involved in healing ministry for more than twenty-eight years. His conviction to pray for healing came in 1989 when his sister, Julie Sheldon, a ballet dancer with the Royal Ballet in London, was healed by God through the late Canon Jim Glennon.

In 2007, Nigel created WELCOME HOME INITIATIVE® services, a program of healing for veterans. The program invites men and women of our armed forces who have served in combat to come free of charge and be "welcomed home." Our focus is on healing for post-traumatic stress and moral injury.

Nigel regularly contributes articles to the *Sharing Magazine*. His ministry has been reported by the *New York Times* as well as broadcast on the *700 Club* and K-Love radio. Nigel has been honored to speak at many seminaries around the United States and the United Kingdom. He has served on the advisory board of Christian Healing Ministries in Jacksonville, Florida, and on the board of directors for the Order of St. Luke.

Nigel enjoys boating, writing, playing the violin, and spending time with his grandchildren. He and his wife, Lynn, live in Virginia Beach, Virginia.

www.byhiswoundsministry.org